Success in Science

Alan McMurdo
Ruth Wylie
Series Editor: Jayne de Courcy

Ages 9–11

BOOK 4

Contents

Introduction 2
1 Living things and their habitats 4
2 Food chains 8
National Test Questions 1 12
3 Forces: gravity and friction 16
4 Balanced and unbalanced forces 20
National Test Questions 2 24
5 Rocks and soils 28
6 Being scientific 32
National Test Questions 3 37
Answers and Guidance 42

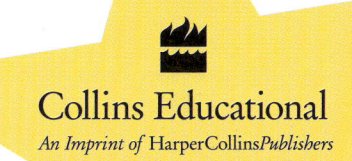

Collins Educational
An Imprint of HarperCollinsPublishers

The 3 Steps to Success ...

Step 1: Coverage of key topics

★ *Success in Science Book 4* covers a number of important Science topics. These topics are ones that your child needs to understand in order to achieve the highest possible level in the Science National Test at the end of Key Stage 2.

★ Each chapter takes one topic and works through it clearly using lots of diagrams and photographs.

★ At the end of each chapter there is a *Test yourself* section with questions to answer. These questions will show how well your child has understood what has been taught.

Step 2: Practice with National Test Questions

★ The book contains three sections of *National Test Questions*. These are past Test questions on the topics covered in the chapters.

★ Your child can do these Test questions immediately after working on the chapters. You might, however, prefer to wait and ask your child to do them a little later to check that the topics have been thoroughly mastered.

Step 3: Improving your child's performance

★ The book contains *Answers and Guidance* to both the *Test yourself* sections and the *National Test Questions*.

★ The authors, both of whom are KS2 Test markers, provide detailed guidance and show how to go about answering the questions in the best possible way.

★ In this way, you can work with your child to improve his/her knowledge and performance in the KS2 Science National Test.

Help with timing

★ As the Science National Test papers are timed, it is important that your child learns to answer questions within a time limit.

★ Each *Test yourself* section and each *National Test Questions* section gives target times for answering the questions. If you choose to, you can ask your child to time himself/herself when answering the questions. You can then compare his/her time against the target times provided in the *Answers and Guidance*. In this way, you will form a good idea of whether your child is working at the right rate to complete the Science National Test papers successfully.

Progression

★ *Success in Science* is aimed at 9–11 year-olds who are in Years 5 and 6 of primary school. Books 1 and 2 cover topics that children are normally taught in school in Year 5 (ages 9/10). Books 3 and 4 cover topics that children are normally taught in school in Year 6 (ages 10/11).

★ To get the most out of *Success in Science*, it is important that your child works through all four books in sequence. If you are buying this series for your child who is already in Year 6, then it is still advisable to work through from Book 1 to Book 4, to ensure that your child benefits from the progression built into the series.

Note to teachers

★ This book, and the other three titles in the *Success in Science* series, are designed for use at home and in schools in Years 5 and 6. They focus on the key science concepts and skills that will raise children's performance in the Science National Test.

★ You can use the books in class or give them to children for homework to ensure that they are fully prepared for their Science National Test.

1 Living things and their habitats

What you need to know
- ★ What do all living things do?
- ★ What is a habitat?
- ★ How are animals and plants suited to their habitat?
- ★ How can we use keys to help us identify animals or plants in a habitat?

This chapter will help you to answer these key questions.

What all animals do

Human beings may seem very different from elephants. We don't have big ears or a trunk! However, we are similar to elephants and all other living animals in some ways. We all need to do certain things to keep alive. We call these **life processes**.

All animals need to **eat** and **drink** to stay alive. What we eat may be different, but the process of **nutrition** is essential for all animals.

All animals **move**. Animals may move in different ways, by flying, crawling, burrowing or walking, but all animals move in some way.

All animals **grow**. Every animal grows as it develops from being young to becoming an adult.

All animals **reproduce**. To reproduce is the scientific word for having babies or offspring. Imagine if one type of animal or plant could not produce the next generation. Eventually, as all the old ones died, there would be no living things of that type left. That is what happens when an animal or plant becomes **extinct**

What all plants do

Plants are similar in some ways to animals because, like animals, all plants:

- need food and water
- grow
- reproduce

Plants do not feed and drink in the same way as animals, but they do need food and water. They make their own food using the energy from sunlight and the water and air around them. There is more about plants, animals and food in Chapter 2.

Plants are different from animals because they do not move as animals do.

Habitats and ecosystems

A **habitat** is the type of place where a particular animal or plant lives. For example, the habitat of a frog might be a pond and its surrounding area. The habitat of a fox might be a wood.

An **ecosystem** contains the habitats for a set of animals and plants and the relationships between the plants and animals that live in them.

Adaptations for habitats

Animals and plants are often specially **adapted** to live successfully in their habitat. Their bodies have certain characteristics that help them. For example, squirrels have strong sharp claws to help them grip the trunks of trees while climbing. They have a long, bushy tail to help them balance and strong back legs to help them jump a long way.

An otter has a long, streamlined body to help it move through the water easily. It uses its large, flat tail to push itself through the water. Its thick, dense coat is waterproof and helps to keep it warm when in the water.

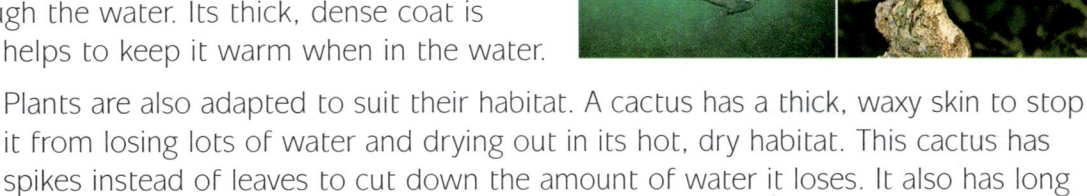

Plants are also adapted to suit their habitat. A cactus has a thick, waxy skin to stop it from losing lots of water and drying out in its hot, dry habitat. This cactus has spikes instead of leaves to cut down the amount of water it loses. It also has long roots that go deep into the ground to take up water.

Caddis fly larva

Tadpole

Using keys to identify animals and plants

There are millions of animals and plants living in the world. It would be impossible for anyone to be able to recognise each and every animal and plant without using a guide to help them.

Classification keys can be used to sort animals and plants and help identify them. Here is an example of a classification key used to sort some creatures found in a pond.

Great diving beetle larva

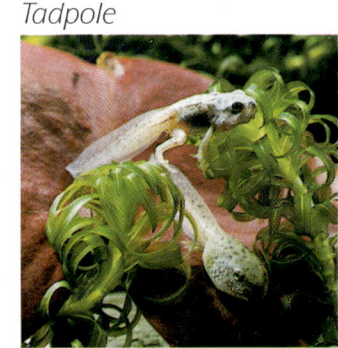

Pond snail

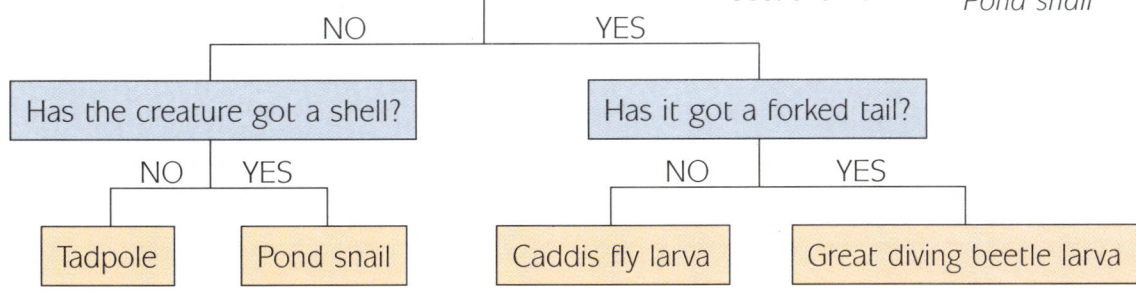

```
                    Has it got 6 legs?
                   NO            YES
         ┌──────────┘              └──────────┐
Has the creature got a shell?    Has it got a forked tail?
     NO        YES                    NO          YES
      │         │                      │            │
   Tadpole  Pond snail          Caddis fly larva  Great diving beetle larva
```

A classification key is made up of a series of 'yes or no' questions based on features that you can see on the living things. You are not asked about features that you cannot see or that do not have a straightforward answer. For example, you cannot answer 'Has it got a long tail?' unless you know how long a long tail is!

To use the key, choose the photograph of one of the animals. Then work through the first question by looking carefully at the animal's features. If the answer is 'yes' go down the yes route to the question about the tail. If the answer is 'no' then go left towards the shell question. By answering 'yes' or 'no' to each question you will eventually end up with the name of your chosen creature.

Using your knowledge

What birds can be identified from a sea shore habitat?

Some children have been on a school field trip to study a seashore habitat. They have collected some pictures of some of the birds they saw. They are trying to make a classification key to help people identify them.

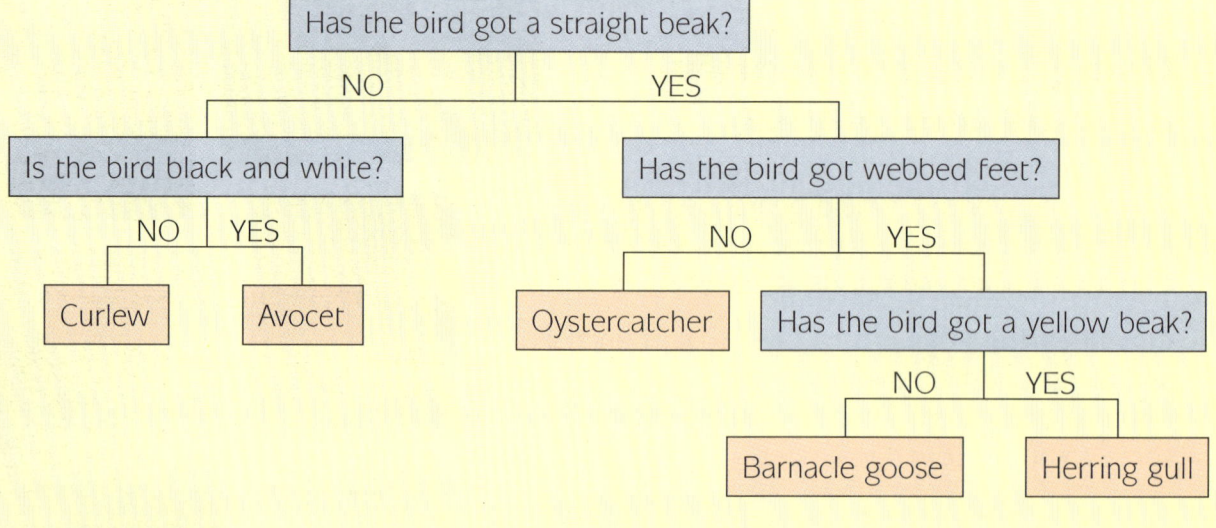

A B C D E

Has the bird got a straight beak?
- NO
  - Is the bird black and white?
    - NO → Curlew
    - YES → Avocet
- YES
  - Has the bird got webbed feet?
    - NO → Oystercatcher
    - YES
      - Has the bird got a yellow beak?
        - NO → Barnacle goose
        - YES → Herring gull

- Can you identify the birds?

Sometimes it can help to write down which of the animals (or plants) fit the 'yes' category and which fit the 'no' category at each split in the key.

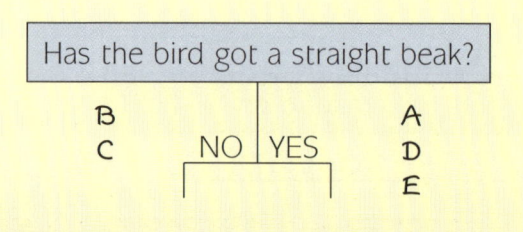

Has the bird got a straight beak?
NO: B, C
YES: A, D, E

6

Test yourself

1 Which three things do all animals do? Tick three boxes.

Run ☐   Swim ☐   Grow ☐

Reproduce ☐   Talk ☐   Move ☐

2 Name two processes that all living things carry out.

3 Match up the word with its meaning by joining the boxes.

Habitat	Where a set of animals and plants live, and the relationships between them
Ecosystem	How an animal or plant is suited to live in its habitat
Adaptation	The type of place where an animal or plant lives

4 Look back at the picture of an otter on page 5. Explain one way that the otter is adapted to move in water.

5 Look at the pictures of frogs. Suggest one way in which a frog is suited to moving in water.

6 Marram grass is a plant that grows on sand dunes. Its habitat is dry because any rainfall drains away quickly. The sand also moves about a great deal in the wind. From this information, name one adaptation you would expect to find in the marram grass and explain why it has this special characteristic.

7 Look again at the key the children used in *Using your knowledge*.

   a How many of the birds had a straight beak?

   b How many of these did not have webbed feet?

Answers and Guidance are given on p.42.   **How long did you take?**

2 Food chains

What you need to know
- What is a food chain?
- What is a producer?
- What is a consumer?
- What are predators and prey?
- What might happen if a food chain is altered?

This chapter will help you to answer these key questions.

Food chains

A **food chain** is a diagram that shows 'what eats what'. The most simple food chains are made up of a plant and two animals. The plant is eaten by one of the animals.

In the first example the grass is eaten by the rabbit. The next step in the food chain shows that this animal gets eaten by another animal. Here the rabbit gets eaten by a fox.

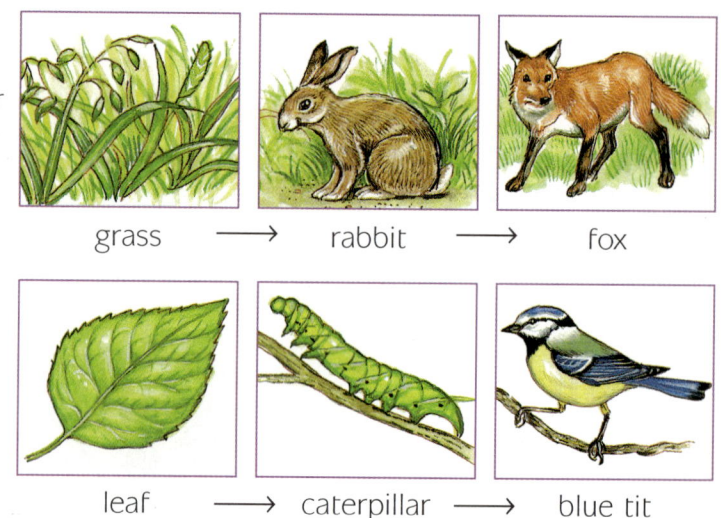

The arrows are important because they show the direction that the **energy** in the food travels. So the energy that is in the leaves goes to the caterpillar. The energy in the caterpillar goes to the blue tit.

Each part of the food chain has a special name.

grass ⟶ rabbit ⟶ fox

leaf ⟶ caterpillar ⟶ blue tit

Producers

At the start of a food chain there is always a green plant. Plants are able use the energy from sunlight to make their own food from water and the air around them. No animal, not even humans, can do this! Only plants can produce their own food. That is why the plant that starts the food chain is called a **producer**. Sometimes the chain may start with part of a plant like a nut or a leaf. Leaves, nuts, berries and other plant parts that animals may feed on have all been produced by plants.

The boxes below contain examples of producers. The plant is the producer even if just part of the plant is eaten.

Grass could be eaten by:	A beech nut could be eaten by:	An apple could be eaten by:
• a rabbit • a cow • a sheep	• a squirrel • a mouse • a vole	• a blue tit • a maggot • a mouse
producer = grass	*producer = beech tree*	*producer = apple tree*

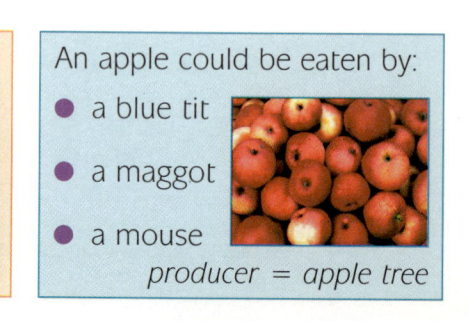

Consumers

A **consumer** is any animal that eats something else. Animals cannot make their own food from sunlight, air and water. So all animals, including humans, are consumers. A consumer may eat a producer or another consumer.

Giraffe = Consumer
The giraffe is eating leaves (leaves are from a producer)

Owl = Consumer
The owl is eating a mouse (another consumer)

Lion = Consumer
The lion is eating a gazelle (another consumer)

Some consumers can only eat producers (plants). We call this type of animal a **herbivore**. Giraffes, sheep and cows are examples of herbivores.

Some consumers eat other consumers (other animals). We call this type of animal a **carnivore**. Lions, tigers and foxes are examples of carnivores.

A consumer that can eat plants and other animals is called an **omnivore**. Pigs and humans are examples of omnivores.

Herbivores    *Carnivore*    *Omnivores*

Predators and prey

Many animals kill other animals and eat them. We call animals that catch and kill other animals **predators**. The animal that gets eaten also has a special name. We call it the **prey**.

Food chains in action

Here is an example of a food chain with four steps. The producer, consumers, predators and prey have been labelled.

producer — *consumer & prey* — *consumer & predator & prey* — *consumer & predator*

rose bush ⟶ aphid (green fly) ⟶ spider ⟶ blue tit

In this example, the spider is a predator because it kills and eats the aphids. But it is also the prey of the blue tit.

Changing food chains

A food chain can change if something happens to affect one step of the chain. For example, if a disease spreads it might kill many animals in one step of the food chain. This happened in the 1950s when myxomatosis, an infectious disease in rabbits, spread through the countryside killing many rabbits. The change in numbers in one step of the food chain had a big effect on another part. When the numbers of rabbits dropped, some foxes starved and others survived by killing and eating different animals, such as pheasants and other birds.

grass   rabbit   fox

pheasants and other birds

Using your knowledge

What can a database tell us about a pond habitat?

Some children researched a database to find out about the plant and animal life in a pond habitat. There was a record for each plant and animal found in the habitat.

DATABASE
Animal: Tadpole [Amphibian]
Description: A young form of a frog, hatched from frog spawn. The tadpole is approximately 2 cm long and grey/brown/black in colour. Tadpoles of the common frog take about 12 weeks to change to the adult form.
Food: Pond weed including Elodea and blanketweed, algae.
Location: In plant cover at the top of the pond.

DATABASE
Plant: Elodea [Flowering plant]
Description: A pond weed that grows in the shallow areas of ponds. It has short, green, curly leaves and tiny purple flowers.
Food: Elodea use light energy to make its own food using water and air dissolved in water.
Location: Rooted at a depth of 30–60 cm but totally submerged under water.

DATABASE
Animal: Great diving beetle [Insect]
Description: A dark green/black beetle, approximately 3 cm in length. The beetle can dive to the bottom of ponds and swim quickly.
Food: Kills and eats other smaller creatures such as water fleas and tadpoles.
Location: Found in the middle depths of the pond at 3–100 cm, although capable of flight.

DATABASE
Animal: Water flea [Crustacea]
Description: A small, usually transparent creature that is very common. Ranges in size from 0.5 to 4 mm depending on type.
Food: Microscopic algae and Elodea.
Location: Found at the pond surface and in open water towards the middle of the pond.

The children used the database to name a producer found in the pond habitat.

- Can you find the producer?
- They also used it to name a predator found in the pond habitat. Can you?

Elodea, the pond weed, is the producer. The great diving beetle kills and eats tadpoles and water fleas, so it is a predator.

They then used the database to write a food chain that might be found in the pond habitat. They found one possible chain:

Elodea (pond weed) ⟶ Water flea ⟶ Great diving beetle

- Can you find another food chain?

Another food chain could be:

Elodea (pond weed) ⟶ Tadpole ⟶ Great diving beetle

Both chains start with Elodea and finish with the great diving beetle.

Test yourself

1. Why do all food chains start with a plant?

2. Linda and Adrian were having an argument about the arrows in a food chain. Linda said 'The direction of the arrows tells you which way the energy in the food flows.' Adrian said 'No, the arrows point to where the food comes from.' Who was right?

3. Look at this food chain.

   cabbage ⟶ snail ⟶ thrush ⟶ sparrow hawk

   a Name a consumer from the food chain that eats plants.
   b Name a consumer from the food chain that eats a predator.
   c Name a consumer from the food chain that is not the prey of any other animal.

4. Hedgehogs also eat snails, and are eaten by sparrow hawks. What might happen to the number of hedgehogs if all the thrushes were to die out?

5. Look again at the database in *Using your knowledge*. Put a tick in the correct box to match up the descriptions with each of the living things in the chain.

Producer	Consumer	Predator	Prey
Water flea			
Elodea			
Great diving beetle			
Tadpole			

Answers and Guidance are given on p.42.   How long did you take?

National Test Questions 1

You should be able to complete these questions in 12 minutes

1 (a) The owl has caught a mouse to feed its young. The owl has good hearing for finding prey at night. Look at the picture.

How else is the owl suited to **catching** its prey?

....

1 mark

(b) Which three things do **all** animals do?

Tick **THREE** boxes.

move ☐   grow ☐

play ☐   walk ☐

wash ☐   reproduce ☐

3 marks

National Test Questions 1

(c) This key describes the skulls of some small animals that owls eat.

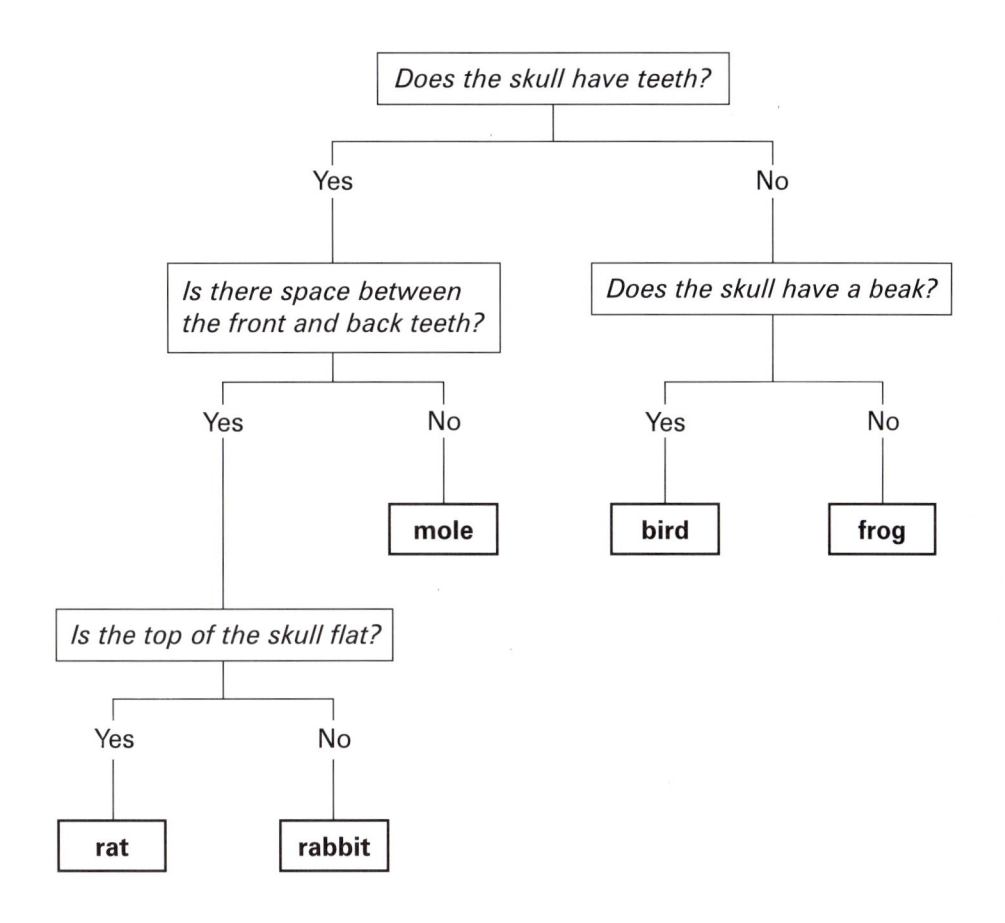

```
                    Does the skull have teeth?
                   /                          \
                 Yes                           No
                 /                              \
   Is there space between            Does the skull have a beak?
   the front and back teeth?          /                    \
        /         \                  Yes                    No
      Yes          No                 |                      |
       |           |                 bird                   frog
       |          mole
  Is the top of the skull flat?
       /         \
      Yes         No
       |           |
      rat        rabbit
```

Use the key to identify the skulls shown below.

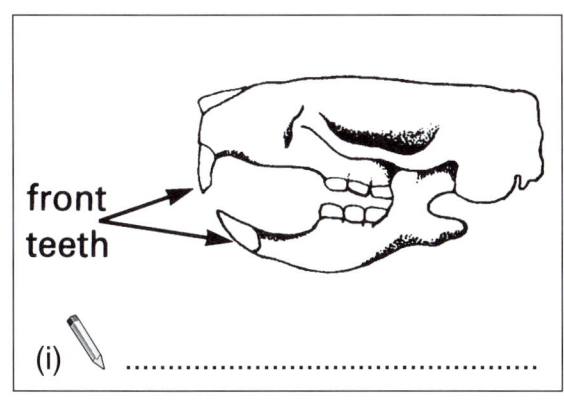

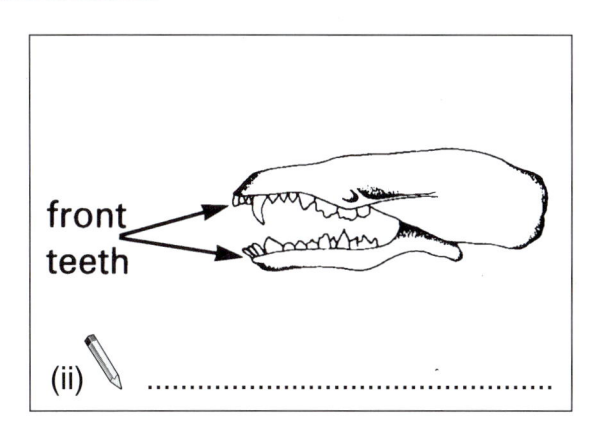

(i) front teeth ....

(ii) front teeth ....

2 marks

1998 B4

13

National Test Questions 1

2 **(a)** These animals live in a freshwater river.

duck

salmon

otter

The otter has a strong tail which it uses to push itself through water.

What part of their body do these animals use to push themselves through the water?

(i) duck ....
1 mark

(ii) salmon ....
1 mark

(b) Here is a food chain from the same river.

algae (*green plants*) ⟶ **water insects** ⟶ **salmon** ⟶ **otters**

Which is the **producer** in this food chain?

....
1 mark

(c) What would be the effect on the number of otters in this river if **ALL** the water insects died?

....
1 mark

1998 B1

National Test Questions 1

3 (a) The pictures show what some of the living things in a pond eat.

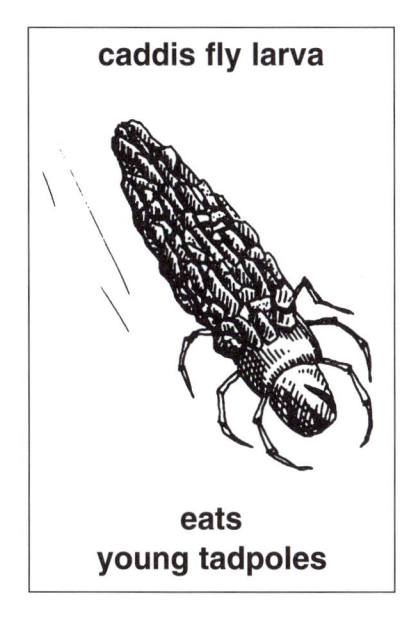

caddis fly larva	young tadpole	great diving beetle larva
eats young tadpoles	eats green plants	eats young tadpoles

Use the information in the pictures.

Write the names of three living things to show one food chain in this pond.

.... → .... → ....

1 mark

(b) Write in the table the names of **ONE** predator, **ONE** prey and **ONE** producer shown in the pictures.

predator	prey	producer
....	....	....

1 mark

1997 B1

Answers and Guidance are given on p.46. How long did you take?

3 Forces: gravity and friction

What you need to know
- What is the force called gravity?
- What is weight?
- Why is weight different for different objects?
- What is friction?
- How can friction be useful to us?
- Why can friction cause us problems?
- What is air resistance?

This chapter will help you to answer these key questions.

The force of gravity

It is hard to believe, but there is a force of attraction between every object. In fact there is a force of attraction between you and everything in the room you are in! However, these forces are usually so small that you cannot feel them.

The more **mass** something has the stronger its force of attraction. Mass is the amount of stuff in an object and is measured in kilograms (kg). It is not a force.

The biggest thing on our world is the Earth itself. The Earth has a big force of attraction and pulls everything towards its centre. This force of attraction is called **gravity**

England is in the northern hemisphere. Have you ever wondered why the people in Australia, on the opposite side of the world, do not fall off the world into space? People all over the world are all pulled towards the centre of the Earth by gravity.

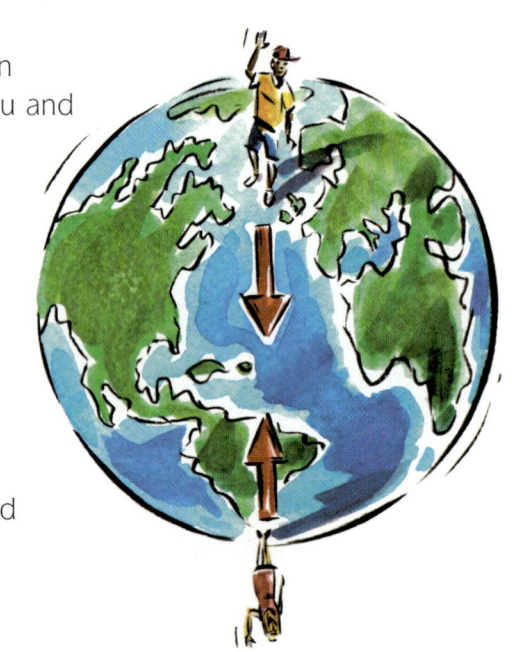

Weight

Weight is the downward force caused by gravity acting on an object. Like all forces, weight is measured in **newtons**.
A **forcemeter** is used to measure the downwards force caused by gravity. In the picture the teddy bear has weight of 4 newtons (4N).

If you cannot remember how to use a forcemeter look back at Book 2, Chapter 6.

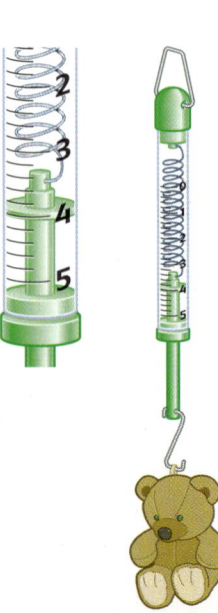

BEWARE!

A common mistake is to mix up mass and weight.

Mass is the amount of 'stuff' in an object and is measured in **kilograms** (kg) It is **not** a force.

Weight is the **downward force caused by gravity** acting on an object.
It is measured in **newtons**.

Why different objects have different weights

The downward pull of gravity does not change. Every kilogram mass of an object is pulled towards the centre of the Earth by the same amount. However, the bigger the mass of an object, the bigger its weight, even though the pull of gravity itself does not change.

A boy measures the downwards pull of gravity on a Lego house. It has a weight of 3N. He then makes another identical house and joins them together. He measures the weight again. The weight is now 6N. There is twice as much mass in the two joined-up houses so the weight, which measures the downward force caused by gravity, is twice as much.

So different objects have different weights depending on their mass.

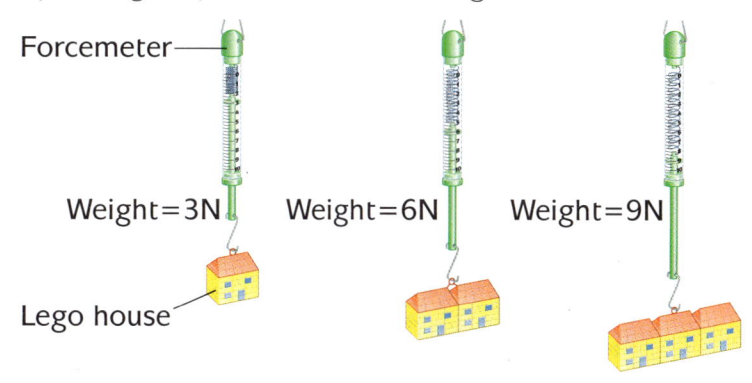

The downwards force caused by gravity is 3N on each house. Gravity does not change but the weight, which is the overall downward pull on the object, does.

The force of friction

Friction is the force that is present between two touching surfaces when one or both of them is moving.

If you give a toy car a push across the playground, it is the force of friction that eventually stops the car moving. The friction occurs as the wheels of the car rub against the ground. Rough surfaces have a higher force of friction than smooth surfaces. There is also some friction between the spinning axle and the car body.

The force of friction is very important and it affects us a great deal in every day life. It can be a very useful force but sometimes it can also cause us problems.

Friction – a useful force

We use the force of friction to give us grip. Mountain bike tyres have large rubber treads to help the bike get through slippery, muddy ground easily. The big tread makes a high force of friction as it rubs against the ground.

We also use big rubber treads on walking shoes to help us grip. When we are walking on steep hills or on a rough path we need a good grip to help us. These walking shoes have a sole made from rubber. Rubber makes a high force of friction when it rubs against other surfaces. The tread is also designed to have a good grip because there is more surface area to increase the friction.

Friction – causing us problems

Sometimes friction can be a problem. As two surfaces rub together, one or both of them can get worn away. This is caused by friction between the surfaces. The friction between peoples' shoes and carpet wears away at the carpet. Carpets get worn away where people walk on them most frequently. This is why the middle part of carpets on stairs usually gets worn before the edges. Surfaces that are rubbing together can also get very hot. Car engines have oil in them to stop the parts rubbing together and getting too hot or worn out. We say the oil **lubricates** the engine.

The force of air resistance

Have you ever cycled really fast down a hill? You can feel the air pushing against you. Maybe you bent down over the handlebars to try and reduce the pushing effect of the air.

This air pushing against you is the **air resistance**. It is the force of the air against any moving object. The bigger the surface area moving into the air, the bigger the air resistance. When you bend down over the handlebars of a bike you make your surface area smaller and so the air resistance is less.

Parachutes work using air resistance. Gravity pulls a parachutist towards the Earth and he or she starts to fall downwards. The parachute opens and the air pushes up against the open canopy. The air resistance works against the force of gravity and so the person falls at a slower speed.

The forces of gravity and air resistance are marked on this diagram. At this point in the parachute jump, the force of gravity is bigger than that of the air resistance so the person is still falling, but at a slower speed than if there was no air resistance.

Using your knowledge

What difference does 'road surface' have on how far a toy car can travel?

Some children decided to find out which of the different surfaces they had would make the best road surface for a toy car. They thought the best surface would be the one which allowed the car to travel furthest. They planned this investigation.

The children put the car in the same place on the ramp each time. They measured the distance the car travelled. The ramp surfaces they investigated were: **felt**, **carpet**, **sugar paper** and **polished wood**.

They drew a bar chart of their results.

- Which material was best and which was worst?
- Using your knowledge of friction, can you explain the results?

The car travelled furthest on the polished wood surface. This was because the surface was smooth and there was only a small force of friction.

The surface that was worst was the carpet. The carpet is soft and it was difficult for the car to run freely on the carpet. There was a large force of friction between the car wheels and the carpet.

A bar chart to show the distances travelled by the car for each surface tested

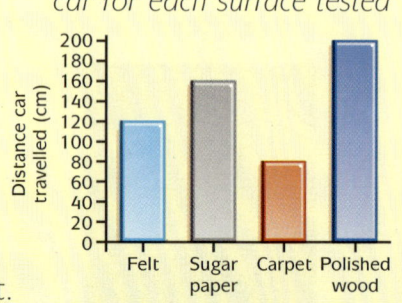

Test yourself

1 Complete these sentences about gravity:

Gravity pulls things towards the ....

The force exerted by gravity is measured in ....

2 When you throw a ball up into the air, what is it that then makes the ball fall to the ground?

3 Put your pen or pencil down. Rub the palms of your hands together. Explain why they get warm.

4 Both these children are wearing shoes with rubber soles. They both have the same size feet. Why does a boot with good grip help when you walk on a slippery surface?

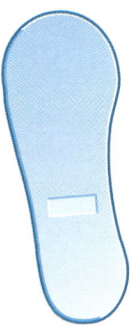

5 Look at these vehicles. If they were all travelling at 40 km/hour, which would have the most air resistance and which would have the least?

lorry   Formula 1 racing car   family car

6 We put oil in the engines of vehicles to cut down on friction. Explain why it is important to do this.

7 In *Using your knowledge*, the children put the four materials they used in order of smoothness:

Roughest ────────────────────────→ Smoothest

carpet   felt   sugar paper   polished wood

Look at these results again. Can you describe a pattern between the smoothness of the material and the distance the car travelled?

Answers and Guidance are given on p.43.   **How long did you take?**

4 Balanced and unbalanced forces

> **What you need to know**
> ★ What do we mean when we say forces are balanced?
> ★ What forces are at work when an object floats?
> ★ What happens to an object if the forces are unbalanced?
> ★ How do forces affect our everyday life?
>
> This chapter will help you to answer these key questions.

Balanced forces

We found out in the last chapter and in Chapter 6 of Book 2 that more than one force can act on an object at any one time. If the forces work against each other in such a way that they cancel out the effect of each other, we say the forces are **balanced**. They produce no overall effect on the object they are acting on. This means that if the object is still, it will not move. If the object is moving it will continue to move at the same speed and in the same direction.

If you put a mug on the table there are two forces acting on it. One of these forces is the downwards pull of gravity, pulling the mug towards the centre of the Earth. But the mug stays on the table: it does not fall through the table. The table is pushing up on the mug and balancing the force of gravity. This force pushing up is called the **reaction force**. The two forces cancel each other out and the mug remains still. The forces are balanced.

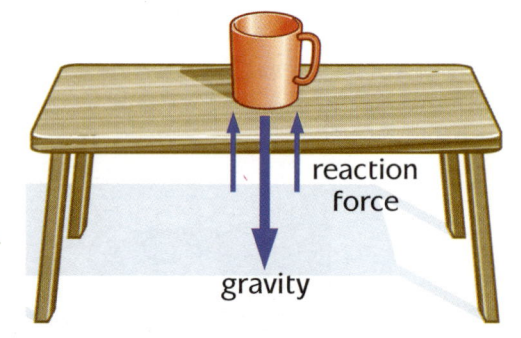

At the start of a tug of war competition, both of the teams have to pick up the rope and 'take the strain' until the flag is positioned exactly in the centre. At this moment the two teams are pulling the same amount, but in opposite directions, and the forces are balanced.

Forces at work when objects float

Even though an object is floating, the force of gravity is still pulling the object down towards the centre of the Earth. (Look back over Chapter 3 if you are still not sure about gravity.) The boat does not sink to the bottom of the tank because the water is pushing up against the bottom of the boat. The pushing up of the water balances the downwards pull of gravity. The two forces are balanced and the boat floats.

We say the pushing-up effect of the water is the **upthrust** of the water. Upthrust is used to describe the pushing-up effect of any liquid.

Unbalanced forces

In Book 2, Chapter 6, we found out that forces can make things speed up, slow down or change direction. They can also make things change shape. The forces in the pictures are all having an effect on an object: they are making it do something (i.e. speed up, change shape, etc.).

If forces act on an object and have an effect, the forces must be **unbalanced** and the object responds to the biggest force. Remember, if the forces working on an object are balanced then there is no overall effect and if the object is still it remains like that and does not move.

The effect of forces on everyday life

This child is floating in the swimming pool. The force of gravity is pulling her down but she does not sink. The upthrust of the water pushes up and balances the downwards force of gravity.

This person is sitting comfortably watching the television. The force of gravity is pulling her down but she does not fall through the chair. The reaction force from the chair balances the downwards force of gravity.

In both of these examples, the forces are balanced and the object, in this case a person, does not move. There is no overall effect from the forces because they are balanced.

This boy has dropped the plate and it has fallen to the floor. The force of gravity pulled the plate down. There was only a very little force pushing against gravity (the push-up from the air: the air resistance) and this was not enough to stop the plate from falling.

This man is lifting up the shopping. The force of gravity is pulling the shopping towards the ground and the force of the person is pulling up on the shopping. At this point the upward force from the person is greater than the downward pull of gravity and the shopping is lifted upwards.

In both of these examples the forces are not balanced and the objects move. There is an overall effect from the forces because they are not balanced.

Using your knowledge

What happens to the weight of things when you put them in water?

A teacher asked some children to find out what happens to the weight of objects when they are placed in water. The children decided to investigate next time they went swimming.

The children chose four waterproof objects. They measured the weight (the downwards force caused by the pull of gravity) of each object in the classroom using a forcemeter. Then they took the objects and the forcemeter to the swimming pool and measured the objects in the water.

Here is a table of their results:

Object	Weight in air	Weight in water
Rubber brick	50 N	30 N
Mug	5 N	3 N
Plasticene ball	2 N	1 N
Apple	2 N	1 N

- Can you describe the pattern in the results?
- What happens to the weight of an object in water and in air?

The weight of the objects is less in water than in air. The pull of gravity appears to be less in water than in air.

In fact, the pull of gravity is **not** less in water. But, in water, the upthrust of the water is pushing up and cancels out some of the effect of the downward pull of gravity.

Test yourself

1 Look at these pictures. There are forces acting on each of the people. Are the forces balanced or unbalanced?

a   b    c

2 Draw the two forces at work on this boat to keep it floating in the water.

3 What are the names of the two forces acting on the boat in question 2?

4 Sort out the following actions into the correct sets, depending on whether they are caused by balanced forces or unbalanced forces:

speed up, **change shape**, **stay the same shape**, **slow down**, **stay still**, **change direction**

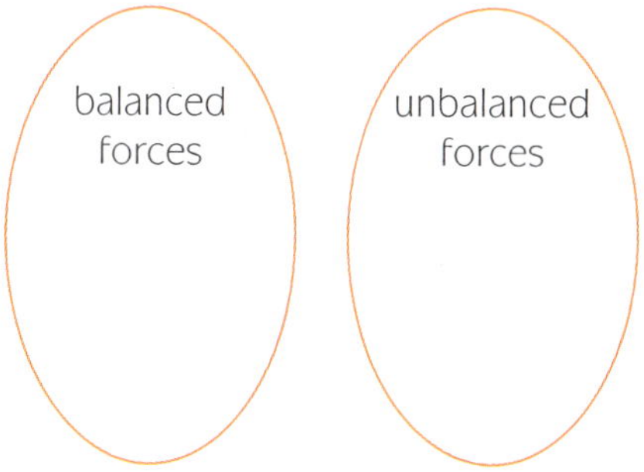

balanced forces   unbalanced forces

5 Are these statements true or false?

a 'As the horse started to trot the cart began to move faster because the forces were balanced.'

b 'When the apple hung from the branch of the tree the force of gravity was greater than the reaction force from the tree branch.'

6 Here is a sketch showing part of a car journey. Fill in the boxes to say whether the forces on the car are balanced or unbalanced.

A car waiting at the traffic lights   the same car speeds up   then it slows down   and it finally stops.

a ▢   b ▢   c ▢   d ▢

7 In *Using your knowledge*, the children found the pattern that objects appear to have less weight in water than in air. Why do you think it was important that they used waterproof objects, rather than, say, a sponge or a book?

Answers and Guidance are given on p.43.   **How long did you take?**

National Test Questions 2

⏱ You should be able to complete these questions in 8 minutes

1 (a) Some children make a plumb line. They tie modelling clay to the end of a piece of string. They use the plumb line to check that things are upright (vertical).

> Explain why the plumb line hangs straight down in a vertical line.

✏ ....

....

1 mark

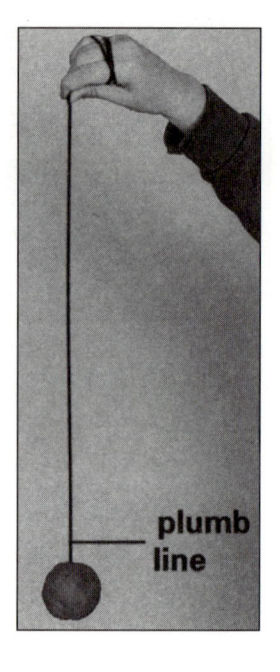

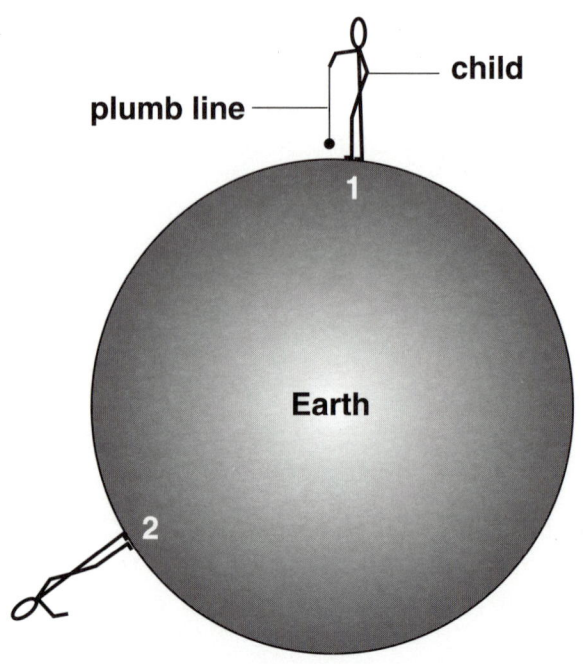

(b) Imagine that two children are holding plumb lines at two different points on the Earth.

The plumb line for the child at point 1 has been drawn for you.

> How would the plumb line for the child at point 2 hang?

Draw the plumb line on the diagram.
1 mark

1998 A10

National Test Questions 2

2 (a) The children have some balloons in the classroom. They have been filled with helium. When Robert lets his balloon go, it rises to the ceiling.

Why does the balloon go up to the ceiling?

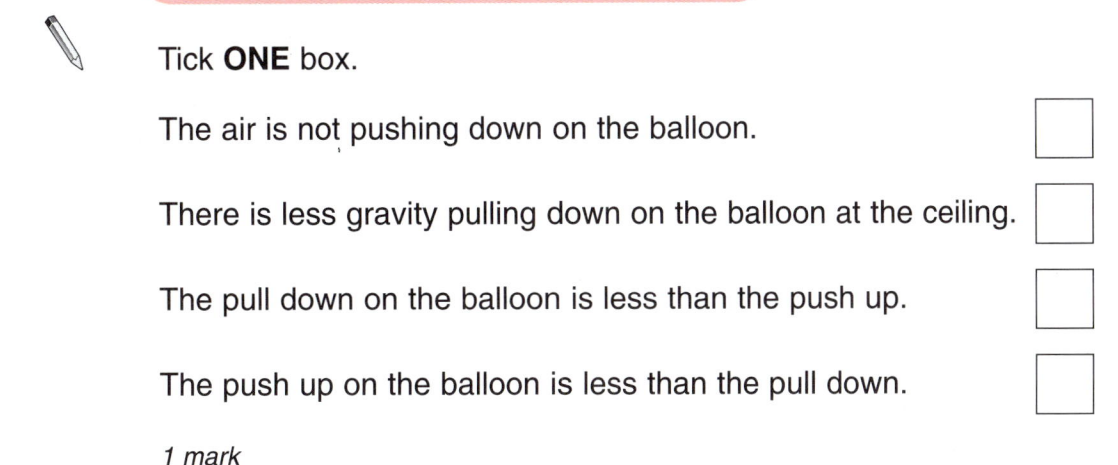

Tick **ONE** box.

The air is not pushing down on the balloon. ☐

There is less gravity pulling down on the balloon at the ceiling. ☐

The pull down on the balloon is less than the push up. ☐

The push up on the balloon is less than the pull down. ☐

1 mark

National Test Questions 2

(b) Hilary puts twelve paperclips on the string of her balloon. The balloon stays at the same height above the floor of the classroom when she lets it go.

Explain why the forces acting on Hilary's balloon, with twelve paper clips on the string, make it stay at the same height.

....

....

1 mark

(c) What will happen to the **movement** of the balloon when she has thirteen paperclips on the string?

....

....

1 mark

(d) Explain your answer to part (c) by describing the **forces** on the balloon.

....

....

1 mark

1998 B10

National Test Questions 2

3 The brick is **not** moving. There is a force up and a force down acting on the brick.

Which statement is correct?

Tick **ONE** box.

☐ The force down is bigger that the force up.

☐ The force up is bigger than the force down.

☐ The force up is the same as the force down.

☐ The force up is twice the force down.

1 mark

1996 A5

4 The children now try to pull the brick along different sorts of flat surfaces (carpet, wood, tiles), and take the readings on the forcemeter each time the brick starts to move.

Which statement is correct and explains their different results?

☐ The force of gravity changes on the different surfaces.

☐ The force that changes each time is the friction between the brick and the surface.

☐ The air resistance stops the brick moving.

☐ The weight of the brick changes on the different surfaces.

1 mark

Answers and Guidance are given on p.46. **How long did you take?**

5 Rocks and soils

What you need to know
- How can we sort and group rocks?
- What is soil?
- Are all soils the same?
- What does the 'permeability' of the soil mean?

This chapter will help you to answer these key questions.

Sorting and grouping rocks

Not all rocks are the same, for example some are really hard and some crumble between your fingers. If you look closely at rocks you will be able to see many differences between them. Here are some of the ways rocks may differ.

Rocks can be many different **colours**:

Mica   *Sandstone*   *Quartz*   *Marble*

Different types of rocks are made up of different **grain** sizes. If you look closely at a rock you can sometimes see the tiny grains of rock that are clumped together to form the stone itself.

Basalt: tiny grains   *Limestone: medium-sized grains*   *Sandstone: large grains*

Rocks may also be sorted by the way they can be split. Rocks such as slate and shale can be split into flat sheets of rock. We say this kind of rock can be **cleaved**

Rocks can also be sorted depending on how well they let water through them. We call this the **permeability** of the rock. Some rocks, such as sandstone, will let water through them easily; they are very permeable. On other rocks, such as marble, the water will sit on the surface or only run off it if they are tilted; these rocks are not permeable.

What soil is made of

Soil is made up of tiny pieces of rock mixed with rotted plants and animals. Soil has been formed over long periods of time, as rock is broken down into smaller and smaller pieces, and mixes with dead and rotting plant and animal material.

If you shake up some soil with water and leave it in a glass jar to settle, you will be able to see all the different parts that make up the soil.

Floating on the top will be leaves and other bits of plant and animal material.

The other layers will show the different types of tiny particles that make up the soil. The heaviest rock particles would drop to the bottom first, then the next heaviest and so on. The top layers of rock particles are the tiny particles of clay and silt. The very top layer is **humus**. Humus is decayed plant and animal material in the soil. It is dark-coloured and adds nutrients to the soil. It does not contain any rock particles.

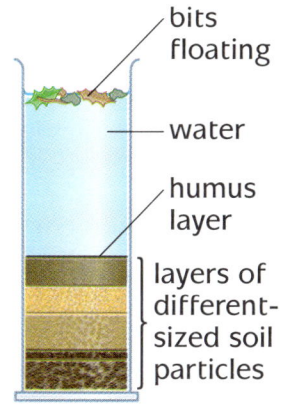

Different soils

Soils can be very different. The kind of soil depends on the type of rock particles that have been broken up to make the soil. The soil also changes depending on the amount of humus.

Red Devon sandy soil

Dark peaty soil

Brown fine loam

Chalky white soil

Look at the photographs of these four different soil types. They look very different: even the colour of the soil varies. The soils would also feel different. Soils that have very small particles of rock in them, for example clay soils, feel much smoother than soils with large gritty grains of rock, for example coarse sandy soil.

The permeability of soils

If something is permeable it means that it is not waterproof, it lets water pass through it. So if soil is permeable it lets water pass through it.

Some soils are more permeable than others. Soils that have big rock grains or particles let the water pass through easily. Soils that have small particles do not let the water pass through easily.

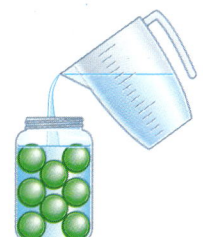

Think of a jam jar full of marbles. The marbles are quite big and there are lots of spaces between them. They do not pack tightly together. If you poured water into the jar it would reach the bottom very quickly because the water can go through the big gaps. Soils with big rock grains behave in this way: the water passes quickly through the spaces between the rock particles.

Now imagine a jar full of tiny beads. The beads would pack very tightly together and there would be little space between them: the gaps would be very small. Soils with small rock particles are just like this and have very small gaps for the water to get through. Water passes through this sort of soil much more slowly.

Using your knowledge

Can soil be used to solve crime?

A group of children read that forensic scientists can sometimes identify criminals from soil samples found on their shoes. Their teacher has set up a detective problem for them to solve.

ROBBERY

A BANK ROBBER has been caught by the police. He is refusing to say where he has buried the stash of money. The bankrobber has muddy shoes, from the field in which he hid the money.

The teacher has brought in a pair of muddy shoes and soil samples from four local fields. By comparing the soil samples with the soil sample from the shoes, the children have to find out which field the owner of the shoes was in.

The children decided to find out what was in the soils by shaking the soils with water.

Here are their results:

Field 1   Field 2   Field 3   Field 4   Muddy shoes

- Can you see which samples match the soil on the shoes?

The children decided that samples from fields 1 and 4 looked quite similar to the soil on the shoes.

- What further test could they do to check the match further?

They tested the permeability of the soils by seeing how much water drained through a funnel full of soil in 5 minutes. They kept it fair by adding 30 ml of water each time.

They made a table of their results:

Soil sample	Amount of water drained through after 5 minutes (cm^3)
Muddy shoes	23
Field 4	16
Field 1	24

The soil from field 1 and the sample from the shoes matched closely: the children had solved the case!

Test yourself

1. Name two ways in which rocks can differ.

2. How is slate different from most other rocks when it is broken?

3. Darren and Jack were having an argument about some scientific words. Darren said that if something is permeable it lets water through, but Jack disagreed. He said that if something is permeable it does not let water through. Who is right, and why?

4. What do we call decomposed plant and animal material in soil?

5. If you were preparing a piece of ground for a sports field and you did not want it to get waterlogged in the rain, would you choose a soil with tiny grains or large grains? Explain your choice.

6. Here is the picture of a jar where the soil has been shaken up with water and then left to settle into layers. Describe the pattern that links the soil particle size and the position of these particles in the jar.

7. In *Using your knowledge*, the results in the permeability test did not match up exactly. The children used 30 ml of water each time, but can you list two other things that the children should have kept the same to make the test fair?

Answers and Guidance are given on p.44.   **How long did you take?**

6 Being scientific

What you need to know
- What is important when planning an investigation?
- What science equipment should I know about?
- What units do I measure in?
- How can I use my results?

This chapter will help you to answer these key questions. Some of your National Test questions will be testing your science **skills**, rather than your knowledge of **facts**.

Planning an investigation

When planning an investigation it is important **to test only one thing at a time**. Everything else that may affect the results has to be kept the same. If you do not do this, the investigation will not be fair.

> Investigation to find out whether the temperature of the water affects how quickly the jelly dissolves.

The thing (**factor**) being investigated is the temperature of the water, so it will be changed. Everything else needs to be the same in each test, because these differences could affect the results. You would not be able to say anything about the effect of temperature if other factors (things that could affect the result) were different.

To plan this investigation you need to answer the following questions:

What am I investigating?

- The temperature of the water (so this is what will be changed).

What will I need to keep the same?

- The amount of jelly used.
- The type of container used.
- The number of stirs given to each container.
- The type (brand) of jelly used.
- The size of bits of solid jelly put in the water.
- The volume of water.

Remember when planning an investigation: only one thing is changed. All the other things that could have an effect need to be kept the same. This must be done to make the investigation a **fair test**.

In a test question, you may be asked to suggest things that should be kept the same to make the investigation fair. Look at the investigation carefully; decide what is being investigated. This is the factor that needs to be changed. Then think about the other things that might affect the results. These are the factors that you should keep the same.

Science equipment

If you come across equipment in your Test paper that you have not seen before, don't panic! There will be information telling you how it works. If you have to read a scale, look carefully and work out how much each step on the scale is worth.

Here are some pieces of science equipment with scales to read:

Measuring cylinder (measures volume of liquid)

Thermometer (measures temperature)

Forcemeter (measures forces)

The thermometer shows that the temperature of the water is 17°C. The large marks show every 5°C and there are five small steps in between (every fifth step is a large mark). This means that each small step is worth 1°C.

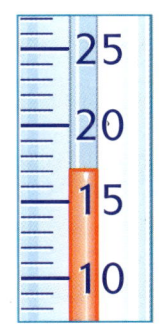

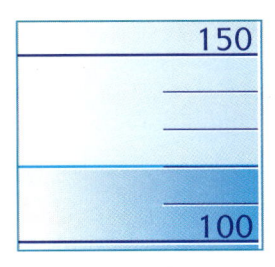

The measuring cylinder has 120 cm^3 of water in it. 100 cm^3 is marked and then each step is another 10 cm^3. So here we have 100 cm^3 + 10 cm^3 + 10 cm^3 = 120 cm^3

Using units to measure

You saw on the scales above that measurements are made and recorded using different units. Here is a list of the most common measurements and their shortened abbreviations.

Measurement of	Unit of measurement
Time	hours (h or hr), minutes (m or min) or seconds (s or sec)
Length	metres (m) or centimetres (cm)
Volume of liquids	centimetres cubed (cm^3) or millilitres (ml)
Temperature	degrees Celsius (°C)
Forces	newtons (N)

Using bar charts

If you look closely at results, you can often see patterns in the information. It is sometimes easier to see these patterns if the results have been put on a graph. This is one of the main reasons for drawing a bar chart or line graph.

A **bar chart** is used when there are different 'things' or groups of 'things' being tested. There will be names of objects or even people along the bottom of the bar chart, and a scale of measurement up the side.

In this example, three children measured their heart beat rate before running for 5 minutes and then measured it again straight after running. From the bar chart you can see a pattern: following exercise, the heart beat rate increased for each child.

A bar chart to show the heart beat rate of each child, before and after exercise

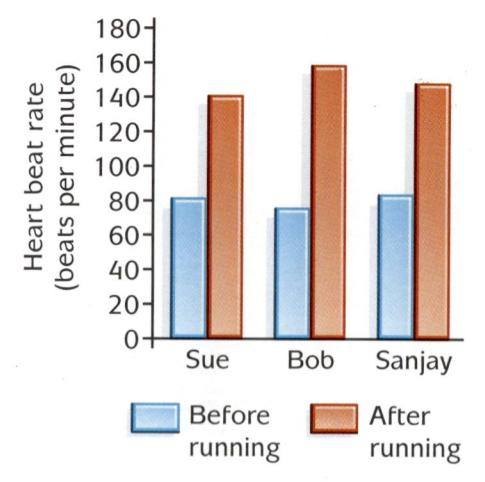

Using line graphs

Look again at the investigation at the start of this chapter. The plan was to find out whether the temperature of the water affected how quickly the jelly dissolved.

Temperature of the water (°C)	Time taken for the jelly to dissolve (sec)
10	100
25	70
40	35
55	20

The results show that both the factor being investigated (the temperature of the water) and the factor being measured (the time taken for the jelly to dissolve) increase continuously and are measured in numbers. If you are investigating something that is measured in numbers, and changes little by little or continuously, then you can draw a **line graph** of the results.

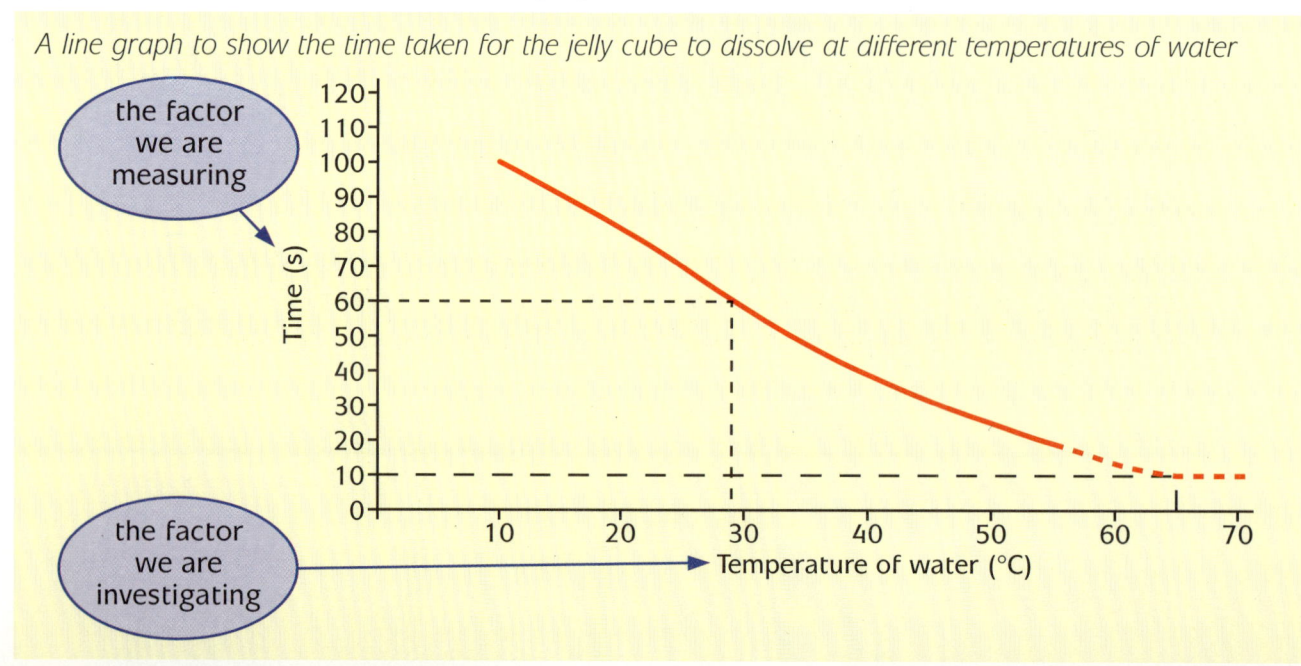

A line graph to show the time taken for the jelly cube to dissolve at different temperatures of water

the factor we are measuring

the factor we are investigating

Finding patterns in results

You can use this line graph to help find patterns in the results. When the water was cold the jelly took a long time to dissolve. When the water was hot the jelly dissolved quickly. The graph shows that there is a link between these two results as there is a smooth line joining the points. So there is a pattern for all the results and you can draw an overall **conclusion** or generalisation:

the hotter the water, the quicker the jelly dissolves

The hotter the water, the quicker the jelly dissolves

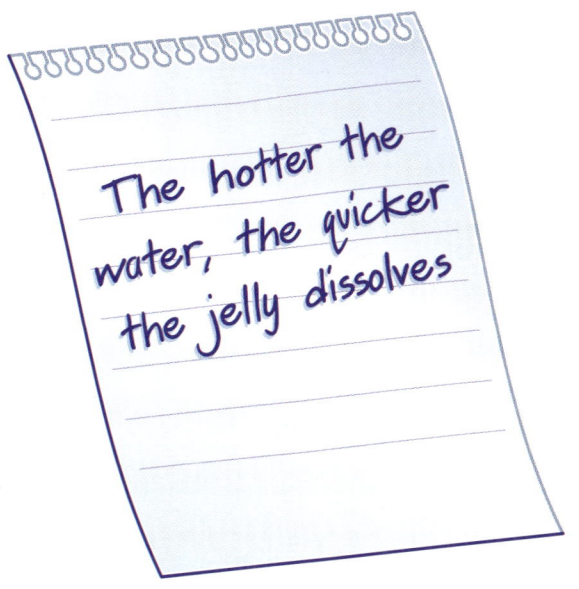

Remember in Book 2 we talked about the 'er' rule. In the conclusion to this jelly investigation we have used the words 'hotter' and 'quicker'.

In all four **Success in Science** books, there have been questions that ask about patterns between results. We have talked about the fact that you need to consider *all* the results. If you said 'the hottest water was the quickest' you are only talking about one result. Even if you said 'the hottest water was quickest and the coldest was slowest' you are only talking about two results and not about all the results in between.

Predicting results

You can also use the line graph to help predict how long it might take the jelly to dissolve at water temperatures that were not tested. If you wanted to predict what would happen at 30°C, go up from 30°C until you reach the curved line and then read across to find out what time it matches. Follow the black dotted lines on the graph. You can predict that at 30°C the jelly will dissolve in about 59 seconds.

You can also extend the line of the graph and carry the curve on. You can use this to predict results for temperatures outside the range of 10°C to 55°C that was tested. For example, at a temperature of 65°C it can be predicted that the jelly will dissolve in about 10 seconds.

Test yourself

1. What is each of these pieces of equipment used to measure?

   a   b   c

2. Complete the table to show what units you would use.

Measurement of	Unit of measurement
Length	
Time	
Forces	
Temperature	
Volume of liquid	

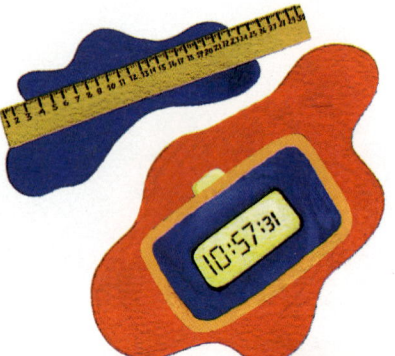

3. Why is it important to do a fair test when trying to find out the effect of something?

4. Here are three investigations. For each set of results, say whether you would draw a bar chart or a line graph with the results.
   a Finding out about the number of children with different eye colours in a class.
   b Finding out the most popular flavour of crisp in the school.
   c Finding out how you heart beat changes over 10 minutes after you have exercised.

5. Look again at the line graph in the jelly investigation. How long do you think it would take the jelly to dissolve in water at:
   a 50°C
   b 5°C?

6. In the jelly investigation the children forgot to record the water temperature for one of the results. They knew the time taken for the jelly to dissolve was 60 seconds but they did not know the water temperature. What is the missing temperature?

Answers and Guidance are given on p.45.   **How long did you take?**

36

National Test Questions 3

You should be able to complete these questions in 13 minutes

1 (a) Jo and Kelly tried scratching rock samples with a fingernail and with steel. A fingernail is quite soft. Steel is hard.

They recorded their results.

Rock	Scratched with	
	fingernail	steel
chalk	✓	✓
flint	✗	✗
granite	✗	✗
sandstone	✗	✓

✓ = made a scratch

✗ = did not make a scratch

Which is the softest rock in the table?

....

1 mark

(b) Use the table to decide if steel is harder than flint.

Tick **ONE** box.

yes ☐   no ☐   maybe ☐   can't tell ☐

1 mark

(c) Explain your answer to part (b).

....

1 mark

(d) Name **ONE** rock in the table which is harder than sandstone.

....

1 mark

1996 A8

National Test Questions 3

2 (a) Children put four different types of soil into funnels. They poured 300 cm³ of water onto each soil. They measured how much water passed through in five minutes.

Look at the picture.

Which soil allowed the least water to pass through it?

Tick **ONE** box.

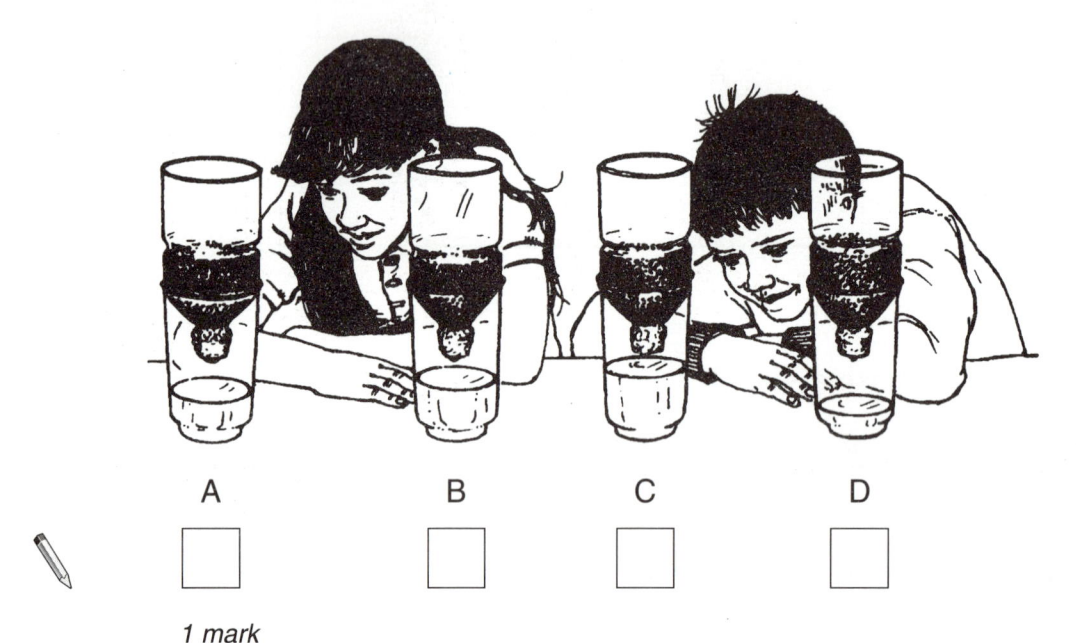

A ☐   B ☐   C ☐   D ☐

1 mark

(b) Clay has small particles and does **not** let water through easily. Sand has larger particles and lets water through easily. The table shows the four types of soil they tested.

Which type of soil was put in each funnel?

Complete the table by writing the letter for each funnel.

soil	funnel
all clay	....
mostly clay, some sand	....
mostly sand, some clay	....
all sand	....

1 mark

(c) The children showed their results on a graph. The graph shows how much water each type of soil let through in five minutes.

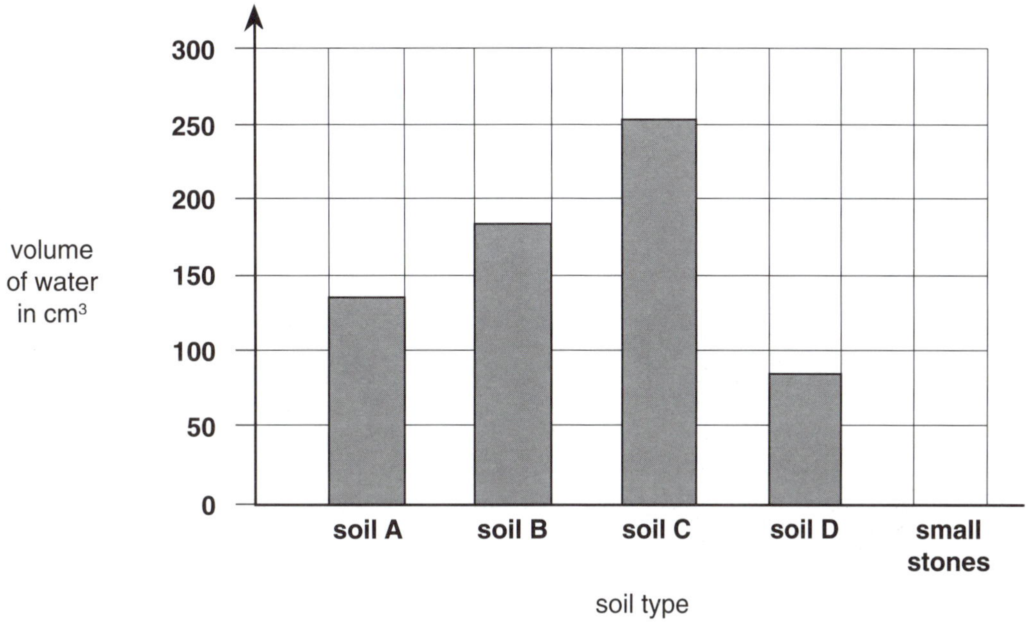
300
250
200
150
100
50
0
volume of water in cm³
soil A
soil B
soil C
soil D
small stones
soil type

The children then poured 300 cm^3 of water onto small stones in a funnel.

Draw a bar on the graph to predict the volume of water which will pass through the small stones in five minutes.

1 mark

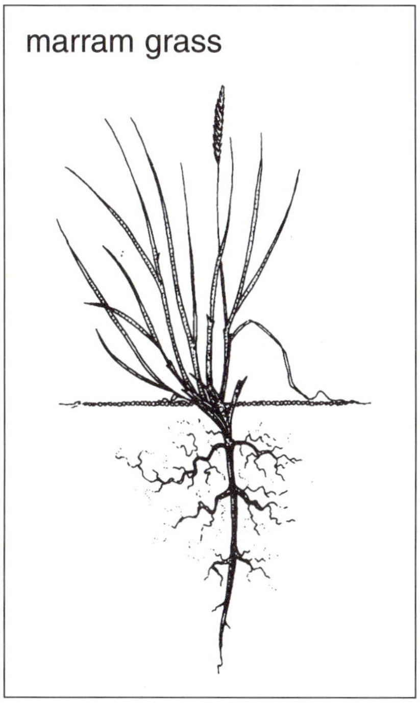
marram grass

(d) Marram grass grows in very sandy places.

Explain how the long roots of the marram grass help it to survive in very sandy places.

....

....

1 mark

1997 A8

National Test Questions 3

3 Jalam saw that the honey ran off the spoon slowly.

Faye put one drop of honey onto a tilted tray. Jalam measured how many seconds the honey took to run 10 cm down the tray.

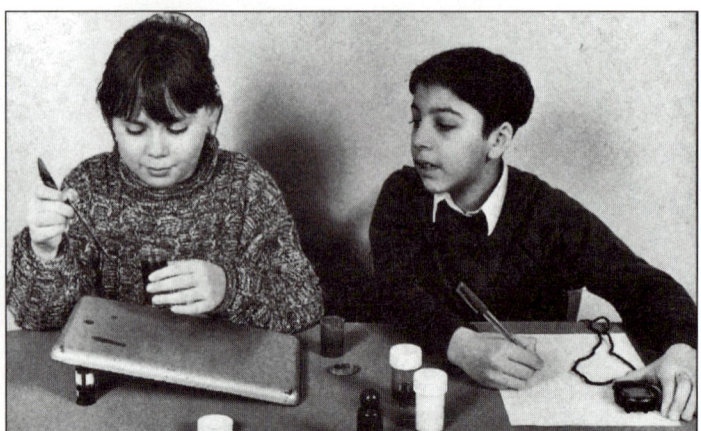

(a) Jalam tested the honey on the tilted tray in the same way, but at different temperatures.

He drew a graph of his results:

Graph to show the effect of temperature on the flow of honey

(y-axis: time taken for honey to run 10 cm in seconds; x-axis: temperature of honey in °C)

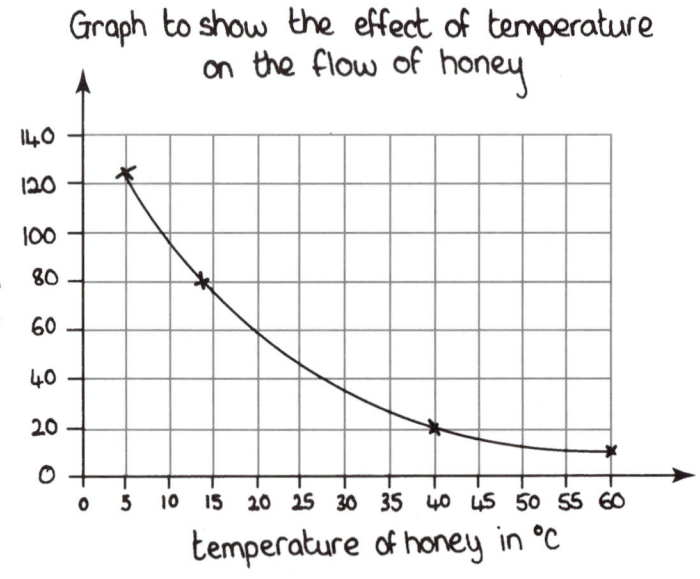

Look at the graph.

How long did it take honey at 40 °C to run 10 cm?

.... seconds.

1 mark

(b) Describe how the time it takes honey to run 10 cm depends on the temperature.

....

2 marks

1998 B7

National Test Questions 3

4

Jill made circuits with different lengths of wire, the same battery and the same bulb. The wire is coated in plastic. She recorded her results in a table.

Look at the table.

length of wire (m)	brightness of light from bulb
40	no light
30	dim glow
20	faint glow
10	bright light
1	very bright light

Describe how changing the length of the wire in the circuit affects the brightness of the light.

....

2 marks

1998 B6

Answers and Guidance are given on p.47. **How long did you take?**

Answers and Guidance

1 Living things and their habitats

1 All animals **reproduce**, **move** and **grow**.

Remember 'all animals' includes a whole range of creatures from worms to crocodiles. The question asked what do all animals do, and you have never seen a worm run!

2 You can choose any two from: **nutrition**, **growth** and **reproduction**

All living things includes both plants and animals. Plants do not move from place to place like animals do.

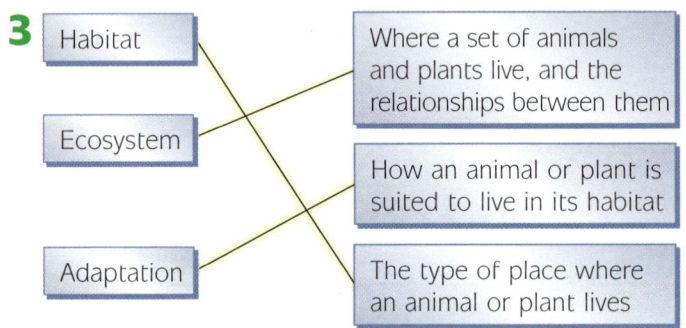

3
- Habitat → The type of place where an animal or plant lives
- Ecosystem → Where a set of animals and plants live, and the relationships between them
- Adaptation → How an animal or plant is suited to live in its habitat

4 You could choose any one of the following: **a long streamlined body to help the otter move easily through the water**, **a large flat tail to help it to swim and change direction** and **waterproof fur.**

5 You could choose any one of the following: **a smooth body to help it move easily through the water**, **webbed back feet to help it to swim** and **strong back legs to help it to swim**.

Other features of a frog may be adaptations to its habitat as well, for example its colour is good camouflage in a pond habitat, but you were asked about adaptations that make the frog suited to moving in water.

6 You could choose any one of the following: **long roots to reach scarce water**, **long roots to anchor it into the shifting sands** and **a type of leaf that cuts down water loss.**

7 a **Three** birds had a straight beak: herring gull, oystercatcher and barnacle goose.

b **One** of these birds did not have webbed feet: oystercatcher.

If you are still not sure, turn back and work through pages 5 and 6 again. If you did not understand the key before, look at it again and see if it makes sense now!

Target time for all questions: 12 minutes

Your time for all questions

2 Food chains

1 **All food chains start with a green plant because they are the only living things that can produce their own food**.

Green plants make their own food. They use the energy from sunlight to make food from water and the air around them.

2 **Linda was right**.

The direction of the arrows in a food chain tells you which way the energy in the food flows. The arrow points to the animal that does the eating. If you start talking about the arrows describing 'what eats what' it becomes very difficult to be clear about what you mean.

3 a **A consumer that eats green plants is the snail**.

b **A consumer that eats a predator is the sparrow hawk**.

A predator is an animal that kills and eats its prey. The only predators in this chain are the thrush (kills and eats snails) and the sparrow hawk (kills and eats thrushes), so it can only be the sparrow hawk that eats another predator.

c **A consumer that is not the prey of any other animal is the sparrow hawk**.

The sparrow hawk is not food for anything else shown in the chain.

4 **If all the thrushes were to die out then the hedgehogs could be affected in two ways. Because there are no thrushes, the sparrow hawks could eat more hedgehogs so the hedgehog numbers could go down. But hedgehogs could also have more snails to eat, because there would not be any thrushes to eat them, so the number of hedgehogs could go up.**

5

	Producer	Consumer	Predator	Prey
Water flea		✓		✓
Elodea	✓			
Great diving beetle		✓	✓	
Tadpole		✓		✓

Target time for all questions: 12 minutes

Your time for all questions

Answers and Guidance

3 Forces: gravity and friction

1 Gravity pulls things towards the **centre of the Earth**.

The force exerted by gravity is measured in **newtons**.

2 **The ball falls to the ground because gravity acts on the ball and pulls it towards the centre of the Earth**.

3 **When you rub the palms of your hands together they get warm because of friction**.

As your hands move over each other there is friction between the two moving surfaces. This friction causes heat to build up so your hands feel warm. Useful on a cold day!

4 **There is more friction between the trainer and the pavement**.

This is because the sole has grooves and ridges on it so its surface area is bigger. This means it creates more friction than the smooth shoe and so it gives better grip. Look again at the question. You are told that both shoes are made of rubber and that they are the same size. As a general rule, if you are told something in the question the answer will be looking for something different.

5 **Most air resistance = lorry.**
Least air resistance = racing car.

Remember the bigger the surface area of the moving object the more air resistance is caused at the same speed. The racing car has a streamlined, smooth design. The less air resistance it has the faster it can go for its engine size.

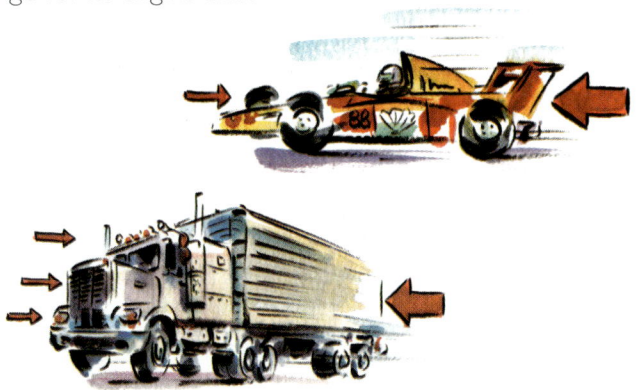

6 **Friction causes the parts inside the engine to heat up and eventually wear out**.

Oil lubricates the inside of the engine and so reduces friction. This means the engine stays cooler and the moving parts do not rub against each other and get worn out.

7 **The smoother the surface the longer the distance travelled**.

You were asked about smoothness and distance travelled. Did you remember to use these two factors, or did you make life complicated? You would be right if you said 'the rougher the surface the less distance travelled' or even 'the smoother the surface the farther it went'. But if you talked about the time the car travelled or the speed the car travelled you would not be right. So, for example, if you said 'the smoother the surface the faster it went' or 'the car went for a long time on the smooth surface' you would not get the marks in a National Test. Nor would you get all the marks you could if you just wrote 'the smoothest went the furthest' or 'the roughest went the shortest'. These answers just tell us about one of the results. They do not tell us the pattern that links all the results.

In Chapter 6 of this book we look at these sorts of questions in greater detail.

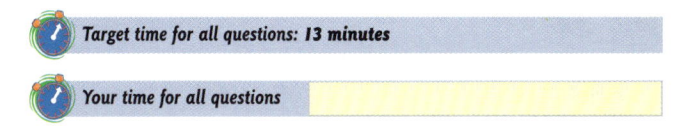

Target time for all questions: 13 minutes

Your time for all questions

4 Balanced and unbalanced forces

1 a **balanced**

The sumo wrestlers are pushing against each other but they are still. The push force from each wrestler cancels the other out and the forces are balanced.

b **balanced**

The person lying on the beach is not moving. The weight of the person (the downwards force caused by gravity) is balanced by the reaction force, the push up from the sand. The forces are balanced.

c **unbalanced**

The sprinter is pushing off the blocks and speeding up. If something is increasing in speed then the forces are not balanced.

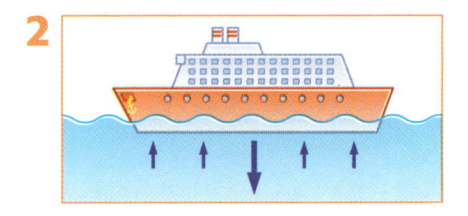

2

Answers and Guidance

3 **The upwards force is called upthrust and the downward force is the weight (the downwards force caused by the pull of gravity).**

When an object is floating the upthrust from the water cancels out the downward pull of gravity and the forces are balanced.

4

- **balanced forces**
  - stay the same shape
  - stay still

- **unbalanced forces**
  - speed up
  - slow down
  - change shape
  - change direction

5 a **False**

If the cart is beginning to move faster it is changing speed. Therefore the pulling force from the horse is greater than the force of friction. The forces are unbalanced.

b **False**

The apple is not moving so the forces are balanced. The downward pull due to gravity is balanced by the pull up force from the tree branch.

6 a **balanced**   **b** **unbalanced**
c **unbalanced**   **d** **balanced**

Remember, if the forces are balanced then there is no change to an object: if it is still it will remain still. If an object changes speed then there is a force which is causing this and the forces are unbalanced.

7 The children were testing the weight of objects in water and air. They had to use waterproof objects because it was important that water was not absorbed into the object. A sponge or book would soak up water and become heavier than when it was full of air. Therefore the test would not be fair, nor would the results be reliable.

Target time for all questions: 15 minutes

Your time for all questions

5 Rocks and soils

1 **Rocks can be different colours, have different grain sizes, different permeabilities and may or may not be split into flat pieces (cleaved).**

2 **Slate can be cleaved into flat sheets whereas most other rocks break into lumps.**

This question asks you for a comparison so make sure you have written about both slate and other rocks in your answer.

3 **Darren was right.**

Something is permeable if it lets water through.

4 **Humus.**

5 **Large grains.**

Large grains let water through far more quickly because they have big gaps or spaces in between them.

6 **The bigger the particles the lower they are in the jar.**

Did you remember to write a pattern that links all the results? If, in a National Test, you had said 'the biggest particles are at the bottom', you would not get full marks because you have only mentioned one result.

7 Two things the children needed to do to make the test fair were:

- have the same amount of soil in each sample
- make sure the soil in all the samples was the same dryness

You could also have said that:

- they needed to use the same size funnel each time
- they needed to pour the water through the funnel at the same speed each time

You could also have made the results more reliable by repeating the tests several times, although this would not make an unfair test any fairer!

Target time for all questions: 12 minutes

Your time for all questions

Answers and Guidance

6 Being scientific

1 a **temperature**

b **force** (Weight is one force that can be measured by a forcemeter.)

c **volume of a liquid**

2

Measurement of	Unit of measurement
Length	**metres (m) or centimetres (cm)**
Time	**hours (h or hr), minutes (m or min) or seconds (s or sec)**
Forces	**newtons (N)**
Temperature	**degrees Celsius (°C)**
Volume of liquid	**centimetres cubed (cm^3) or millilitres (ml)**

3 **If the test is not fair you cannot be sure that your results are due to the thing you are investigating.**

Unless you change just one thing at a time, the other factors could have an effect that you would not know about. So to make it fair, you must only change the factor you are investigating.

4 a **bar chart**

b **bar chart**

c **line graph**

Eye colour and crisp flavours are in groups. A crisp flavour might be salt & vinegar or some other flavour, and eye colours are also in groups or categories like brown and blue. Heart beat and time, however, change little by little or continuously, so a line graph can be drawn.

5 a **22 seconds**

Remember, find the temperature you have been asked about. Go up from this temperature to the curved line and then across to find the time.

b **115 seconds**

To estimate the time taken for the jelly to dissolve at 5°C you need to extend the curved line of the graph. You then need to follow up from 5°C until you reach the curved line and read across to find out how long the jelly will take to dissolve.

6 **29°C**

In this question you were told the time but not the temperature. This is the other way round to question 5, but the process is the same! Find the time you have been asked about. Go across from this time to the curved line and then down to find the temperature.

Target time for all questions: 12 minutes

Your time for all questions

Answers and Guidance

National Test Questions 1

1 a You would score a mark if you gave a specific adaptation of the owl for catching prey, such as **'sharp or long talons'**, **'sharp or long claws'**, **'big eyes'**, **'sharp or strong beak'**.

Some other possible answers are **'it can turn its head round'**, **'it can fly silently'** or **'it can see its prey at night'**. A common mistake made when answering this type of question is to give a general feature of all birds rather than something that helps the owl catch its prey. For example 'it has got a beak', 'it has got claws' or 'it can be quiet' would not get you the mark.

b You should have ticked **move**, **grow** and **reproduce**.

Make sure you follow the instructions: did you tick only three? You get one mark for each correct answer, but will lose marks for an incorrect answer if you ticked more than three.

c (i) **rat** (ii) **mole**

CROSS-CHECK CHAPTER 1

2 a (i) **The duck uses its webbed feet or legs to push itself through the water**.

You would get the mark if you wrote **'feet'**, **'big feet'** or **'muscles'**, but you would not get the mark if you said 'flippers'.

(ii) **The salmon uses its tail or tail fin to move through water**.

Again you would get the mark if you said **'fins'** or **'muscles'** but not if you said 'flippers'. A common mistake is to say 'gills' or 'streamlining'. These are features of a fish but they are not used for pushing it through the water.

b **Algae** or **green plants**.

Remember, only green plants can produce their own food. Notice that the question asked for a producer in the food chain given, so you would not be right if you gave another green plant like grass or oak. Algae are green plants.

c You would get the mark if you gave one way that the loss of food will affect the otters. The best answer is **'there would be fewer otters'**.

There are two stages to go through to get to this answer. If all the water insects died there would be less food for all the salmon, so some of them would starve and die. If the salmon died there would be less food for the otters, so some of them would starve and die.

Other perfectly good answers, and there are lots, include **'the otters would die'**, **'the otters would starve'** and **'the otters would have to live somewhere else'** because all three of these would cause a reduction in the number of otters in the river. Remember to try and keep your answers simple, and based on the information in the question. If, for example, you said, 'the otters would have to eat something else' you might well be right but we do not know whether otters behave like this when they are starving!

There are two common mistakes made by children answering this type of question. The first is to write something that is not to do with the numbers of otters, like 'there'd be less fish' or 'the animals would starve'. The second is to talk about an effect on the otters without being specific about a decrease, for example 'the number of otters would change'.

CROSS-CHECK CHAPTER 1

3 a **green plants ⟶ young tadpoles ⟶ caddis fly larva** or **great diving beetle**

You would only get the mark if you got all three parts right. Did you remember to keep it simple and stick to the information given in the question?

predator	prey	producer
caddis fly larva or **great diving beetle larva**	**(young) tadpole**	**green plant(s)**

b

You would only get the mark if you got all three parts right. The words in brackets are not needed to make the answer correct. In both these questions you would have got the mark if you had said pondweed rather than green plant even though the tadpole eats algae

CROSS-CHECK CHAPTER 2

National Test Questions 2

1 a You would get the mark if you said that a **'force pulls it down'** or **'because of its weight or gravity'**.

Remember that gravity pulls down, and the force caused by gravity is the weight of the modelling clay. So you would get the mark if you said that **'the clay weighs it down'** or that **'the ball is heavy'**. If you did not write about force, you would not get the mark. So for example, 'because of the clay' or 'it hangs down' are wrong.

Answers and Guidance

b You had to draw a line from child 2 pointing towards the centre of the Earth.

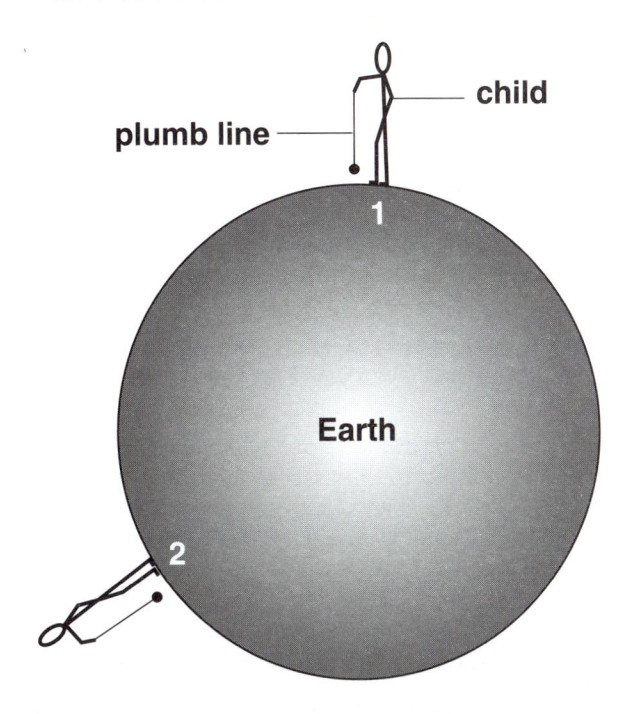

[Diagram: Earth with child 1 standing on top holding a plumb line pointing to centre; child 2 on bottom-left also with plumb line pointing to centre.]

CROSS-CHECK CHAPTER 3

2 a **The pull down on the balloon is less than the push up.**

This question is about unbalanced forces causing the balloon to move upwards.

b **It stays the same height because the forces are balanced.**

The downward pull of gravity is cancelled out by the upward force of the helium in the balloon.

c **The balloon will come down.**

d **The downward force of gravity is bigger than the upward force of the helium in the balloon.**

If there are more paper clips then there will be more mass for gravity to act on. So there will be more downward force. This will mean that the forces are no longer balanced and the balloon will drop towards the floor.

Remember to keep your answer simple. If you said 'it will go down a bit' in part c, what did you really mean? Did you mean that it will go down a little than stop, floating in the air? Or did you mean that it will go down slowly? Perhaps you meant that it will go down a little way then rise again! The person marking your Test paper would not know from this answer which of these three things you meant, and only the second one is right. Help the marker by keeping your answer simple.

CROSS-CHECK CHAPTER 4

3 **The force up is the same as the force down.**

This is a question about balanced forces because you are told that the brick is not moving.

CROSS-CHECK CHAPTER 4

4 **The force that changes each time is the friction between the brick and the surface**

This is a question about unbalanced forces because the children are trying to make the brick move. It is the force of friction that they have to work against to make the brick move. Gravity does not change nor does the weight of the brick.

CROSS-CHECK CHAPTER 4

National Test Questions 3

1 a **Chalk**

Chalk is the only rock than can be scratched by a fingernail, which you are told is softer than steel. Although you might not have covered the hardness of rocks in class, you are given all the information you need in the question.

b **no**

c **Steel did not make a scratch in flint, so steel must be softer than flint.**

d **Flint** or **granite**

From the table you know that sandstone can be scratched by steel. Flint and granite cannot be scratched by steel so they must be harder than steel and therefore harder than sandstone.

CROSS-CHECK CHAPTER 5

Answers and Guidance

2 a D

The water in bottle D was lowest, so soil D must have let the least water through.

b
soil	funnel
all clay	D
mostly clay, some sand	A
mostly sand, some clay	B
all sand	C

The soil with most sand in will let through most water because sand particles are bigger than clay particles. Clay soil, with its tiny particles, will not let through much water at all.

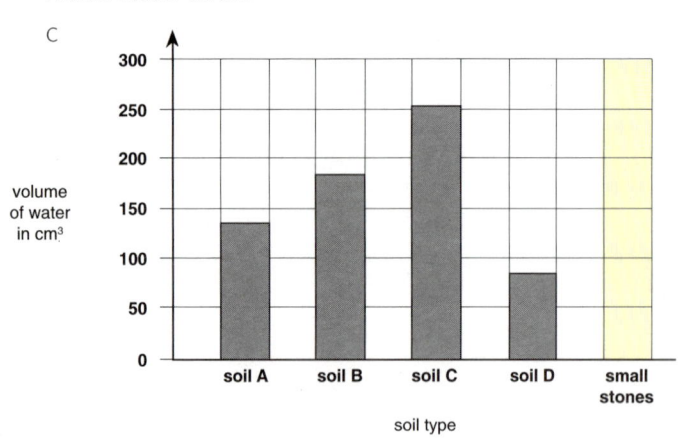

c

Did your bar look like this? You would be right if you drew your bar above 250 cm³ because you know small stones will let through more water than soil C, which is sand. It cannot be more than 300 cm³ because that is how much water the children poured on!

CROSS-CHECK CHAPTER 5

d **Long roots take in or absorb more water and they anchor the plant in the sand**.

You would get the mark for saying either of these things about the roots. You would not get the mark if you described the roots as drinking or sucking up water. Try not to use human actions, like 'finding water' or 'seeking water', to describe what happens in plants.

CROSS-CHECK CHAPTER 1

3 a 20

If you got this wrong look back at the graph. Find 40°C along the bottom, go up to the curved line and then run along to read of the time on the left. It is exactly 20. Also notice that seconds is printed on the question so you do not need to give any unit at all. In fact if you give the wrong one you might lose the mark. So read the question carefully.

b **'The higher the temperature the less time it takes'** or **'the lower the temperature the more time it takes'**.

Either of these statements states a pattern that links all the results. As we have seen throughout *Success in Science*, a pattern has to link all the results. In this question you are asked to compare temperature and time. You might have got the marks if you had talked about speed, for example 'the hotter it is the faster it flows', but why make things complicated? Remember that you will only score one of the marks if you just compare one or two results. For example: 'the coldest took longest' and 'the hottest was fastest' do not describe the full range of results.

CROSS-CHECK CHAPTER 6

4 The longer the wire, the dimmer the light or **the shorter the wire the brighter the light**.

Common mistakes in this question include answers that only compare one or two results, for example 'the shortest was the brightest and the longest was the dimmest'. This answer would only get one mark because the full range of results has not been described. Another mistake is to offer and explanation. 'The longer it is the dimmer it is because the electricity is used up round the circuit' would not get any marks because the science is wrong and an explanation was not asked for. 'The longer it is the more time it takes to get round the circuit' would not get you any marks either, because you have not used the information given in the question. There is more on this in Book 3, Chapter 5.

CROSS-CHECK CHAPTER 6

LONGMAN

WORDS

2

Illustrated by Graham Round

All Round English is a carefully graded course in language. It consists of four course books and five associated workbooks. The first of these workbooks, *Starting With Words*, is designed as an introduction to the course. *Words 1–4* parallel each of the course books and offer lively practice.

LONGMAN GROUP UK LIMITED
Longman House,
Burnt Mill, Harlow, Essex CM20 2JE, England

© R. R. Productions Ltd. 1974.

All rights reserved. No part of this publication may be reproduced, stored in a retrieval system, or transmitted in any form or by any means, electronic, mechanical, photocopying, recording or otherwise, without either the prior written permission of the Publisher or a licence permitting restricted copying issued by the Copyright Licensing Agency Ltd, 90 Tottenham Court Road, London W1P 9HE.

First published 1974
Twenty-second impression 1993
ISBN 0 582 18491 6
Printed in Malaysia by TCP

The publisher's policy is to use paper manufactured from sustainable forests.

£2.25

ISBN 0-582-18491-6

9 780582 184916

RONALD RIDOUT

jockey, a person who rides race horses

knotty, full of knots

larder, a small room for keeping food
learner, a person who learns
least, the smallest in size or amount
lock, a door-catch worked with a key
longest, longer than all the others

mark, a spot
market, a place where you buy things
miner, a person who digs coal
monkey, an animal that chatters
mossy, covered with moss
mouse, an animal that squeaks
muddy, covered in mud

neatest, the most tidy
nothing, not anything

oil, a liquid to make wheels run smoothly

Paisley, a town
Pakistan, a country
panda, an animal
pansy, a flower
Parsons, a surname
park, to leave your car in a special place
part, some but not all of it
Patricia, a girl's name
penguin, a bird
pig, an animal that grunts
Philip, a boy's name
player, a person who plays
plum, a fruit
Porsche, a car
port, a town with a harbour
porter, a person who earns his living by carrying things
potato, a vegetable
pound, a hundred pence
preacher, a person who preaches
press, to push steadily against
pretty, good-looking
purse, a container for money

reach, to stretch out the hand for and take
rear, the back part
robber, a person who steals; a thief

sailing, moving across water
shabby, much worn
shopper, a person who goes shopping
skater, a person who skates
slippers, loose-fitting shoes for indoors
sloppy, messy; not done with care
smart, clean, well-dressed
smelly, having an unpleasant smell
snake, an animal that hisses and glides
sorry, feeling sad because you have done wrong
space, emptiness
spotty, covered in spots
start, to begin
storm, a period of rough wet weather
stormy, full of storms
stubby, short and thick
sunny, full of sunshine
swing, a seat on ropes that goes up and down

talker, a person who talks
tart, a fruit pie
teacher, a person who teaches
tears, drops that come from the eyes when we cry
telly, a short way of saying television
thinnest, thinner than all the others
twice, two times

walker, a person who walks
wetter, not as dry as the others are
whole, unbroken; the complete thing
wing, the arm of a bird
wolf, an animal that howls

THE LITTLE DICTIONARY

Aberdeen, a city
antelope, an animal
apart, aside; separate from
artist, a person who draws or paints pictures
Austria, a country
awake, not asleep
Atkins, a surname

---

baker, a person who bakes bread
barber, a person who cuts hair and shaves
barmy, crazy; mad
barn, a building for storing corn or hay
beach, the shore between low tide and high
biggest, the opposite of smallest
block, a large solid piece of wood
boggy, marshy; wet and muddy
bossy, too fond of giving orders
bull, an animal that bellows

---

cart, vehicle pulled by a horse
chart, a sort of map
chopper, a tool used for chopping meat or wood
chubby, plump
clock, an instrument for showing the time
cock, a bird that crows
cord, a very strong string
cork, a bottle stopper
corn, wheat, oats, barley etc.
corner, a place where two sides meet
cream, food made from milk
cyclist, a person who rides a bicycle

---

darn, to mend a hole in your clothes
dart, a pointed object to throw at a target
deer, an animal that has antlers
dentist, a person who looks after your teeth
depart, to leave
diver, a person who dives
dizzy, feeling as if your head were going round
docker, a person who loads and unloads ships
donkey, an animal that brays
dream, what you seem to see during sleep
duck, a bird that quacks
dozen, twelve

---

early, the opposite of late
earn, to gain money by working
earner, a person who earns money
east, the opposite of west; where the sun rises
easy, not difficult; simple

farm, land for raising crops or cattle
farmer, a person who raises crops or animals
fear, what you feel when there is danger
fizzy, full of small bubbles
flatten, to make flat
flatter, not as hilly as the other land
flower, to come into bloom
fluffy, covered with fur or down
foggy, misty
fort, a strong point built for defence
forty, ten more than thirty; 30×10
frown, to make lines come on the forehead
funny, comical
furry, covered in fur
fussy, making too much fuss

---

garden, land that belongs to a house
groom, a person who looks after horses

---

happy, joyful; not sad
hard, not soft
hear, what you do with your ears
heater, something that warms up a room
hottest, hotter than all the others
hunter, a person who hunts
hurry, to hasten

60 This is to remind you that the same sound is often spelt in different ways. Thus **burn** and **learn** rhyme because **urn** and **earn** have the same sound. Pronounce the following words carefully and then write them under the words they rhyme with.

high   third   soul   mum   hood   some   bite   word
should sky   chum   why   curd   kite   come   write
goal   roll   cry   would   whole   wood   bright heard

bird	pie	hum	light	hole	could

61 If you solve this puzzle correctly, the first column down will spell a couple of very large animals.

1 Two times
2 Unbroken; the complete thing; all of it
3 You use this to make wheels turn easily
4 The opposite of late
5 Larger than all the others
6 To gain money by working
7 A hundred pence
8 To hasten
9 Not asleep
10 Not anything
11 A short way of saying television
12 You wear them on your feet indoors only.

58

When a noun ends in **-y** with a consonant before,
it changes the **y** into **i** and adds **-es**
to make the plural (more than one),
as you can see from these examples:
story—stories   lady—ladies   fly—flies   cherry—cherries

Write in the missing singular or plural of the following nouns:

singular	plural	singular	plural	singular	plural
1 _____	ladies	6 fly	_____	11 _____	lorries
2 _____	babies	7 story	_____	12 lady	_____
3 _____	berries	8 cherry	_____	13 _____	puppies
4 _____	cities	9 baby	_____	14 city	_____
5 _____	cries	10 pony	_____	15 _____	countries

59

When you want to change the ending of a verb, you do it in much the same way.
You change the **-y** into an **i** and add **-es** or **-ed**, as you can see
from these examples: cry, cries, cried   carry, carries, carried
                       try, tries, tried   marry, marries, married
                       dry, dries, dried   hurry, hurries, hurried

How will you complete these sentences? Not all the verbs you need are in the lis

1 Mother usually _____ the clothes out of doors; but today she is drying them indoors.

2 Kevin often _____ to school; he had to hurry this morning.

3 The baby next door often _____; it cried several times yesterday.

4 Ted often fries the bacon; he _____ some for tea yesterday.

5 When Kate _____, she is going to marry a film star.

6 I often tidy my desk; I _____ it twice last week.

7 Mr Lee flew to New York last week; he often _____ there on business.

8 Lesley's pony often shies at unusual jumps; he _____ at three jumps in the show jumping yesterday.

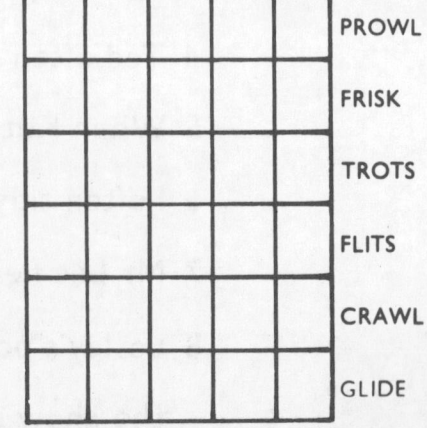

56

Notice what happens when you add **-er** or **-est** to words like this:

big	wet	thin	flat	slim	mad	hot
bigger	wetter	thinner	flatter	slimmer	madder	hotter
biggest	wettest	thinnest	flattest	slimmest	maddest	hottest

Here are some more words formed in the same way:

slip	shop	chop	rob	spin	flat	mad	fat
slipper	shopper	chopper	robber	spinner	flatten	madden	fatten

The words needed to solve this puzzle can be found in the lists above.

1. Thinner than all the others
2. Hotter than all the others
3. Not as dry as the other one
4. The opposite of smallest
5. A person who goes shopping
6. To make flat
7. A tool used for chopping meat or wood
8. A light loose-fitting shoe for indoors
9. A person who steals; a thief
10. Not as hilly as the other land

57

Choose the missing verb from the list.
Write it in the squares.

1 A dog	BLEAT
2 Sheep	PURRS
3 A cat	BARKS
4 A lion	HOOTS
5 An owl	CROAK
6 Frogs	ROARS
7 A donkey	PROWL
8 A bat	FRISK
9 Beetles	TROTS
10 Wolves	FLITS
11 Seagulls	CRAWL
12 Lambs	GLIDE

53

Use each of these words to fill one of the blanks in the sentences.

tried	lies	blew	few	grew	die
tied	lied	drew	knew	pie	died

1 That rogue tells _____; he certainly _____ when he spoke just now

2 Very _____ children _____ that Shakespeare _____ in 1616.

3 Ted _____ a plan on a piece of paper, but the wind _____ it away.

4 Last year Linda _____ a whole inch in six months.

5 In an amusing competition, Mark _____ to eat a _____ without using his hands, and he nearly _____ himself in knots.

6 Flowers soon _____ if they are left without water.

54

In which list will you write each of these?

hump   rope   lump
pencil pole   stub
thread blob   spear
tub   knob   plank
club   stick   mound
        tail

short fat things		long thin things	
1 _____	5 _____	1 _____	5 _____
2 _____	6 _____	2 _____	6 _____
3 _____	7 _____	3 _____	7 _____
4 _____	8 _____	4 _____	8 _____

55

Complete these sentences by choosing the right word to write in the squares.

1 You ☐☐☐☐ kettles of water.   JOIN

2 You ☐☐☐☐☐ hinges to make them quiet.   POINT

3 You ☐☐☐☐ two pieces to make one.   SPOIL

4 You ☐☐☐☐☐☐ with your hand.   BOIL

5 You ☐☐☐☐☐☐ your work by being untidy.   OIL

6 You ☐☐☐☐ ropes to store them.   COIL

51

Notice what happens when you add **-ed** to these words:

| clap—clapped | drop—dropped | fit—fitted | tug—tugged |
| pat—patted | stop—stopped | pin—pinned | rub—rubbed |

Now complete each of these sentences with the best word from the list.

1 When the cyclist came to the red light, he _____.

2 At the end of the concert everyone _____ the actors.

3 When Lucy _____ the glass, it broke into a hundred pieces.

4 The pony came running up, and Wendy _____ it on the neck.

5 Mark _____ on the jeans, but they were much too big.

6 The cat _____ its head against my leg.

7 We _____ so hard that the rope broke.

8 The headmaster _____ up a notice and everyone gathered round to read it.

52

Can you complete these phrases?
Find the missing words in the list.
Write them in the squares.

	of matches	BUNCH
1 a	of matches	BUNCH
2 a	of soup	BAR
3 a	of flowers	PINCH
4 a	of potatoes	SACK
5 a	of chocolate	PAIR
6 a	of shoes	TIN
7 a	of jam	GLASS
8 a	of water	TUFT
9 a	of grass	JAR
10 a	of salt	BOX

25

49

Kevin played a pencil and paper game the other day. He had to find words beginning with A. He was able to get eight in the time allowed. Can you find the other four for him? Then find in the Little Dictionary the 12 words beginning with P.

A

1. A girl's name — Amy
2. A boy's name — Anthony
3. A surname —
4. A vegetable — artichoke
5. A fruit — apple
6. A flower — aster
7. A country —
8. A town or city —
9. A bird — auk
10. An animal —
11. A container — attaché-case
12. A make of car — Austin

50

Notice how these words are made up. Then make new words by placing **a-** or **be-** in front of each of those below:

aside   along   ahead   aware   above
beside   belong   behead   beware   began

1 ____ low   6 ____ lone   11 ____ gin   16 ____ tray
2 ____ live   7 ____ hind   12 ____ way   17 ____ maze
3 ____ gain   8 ____ loud   13 ____ witch   18 ____ cause
4 ____ come   9 ____ fore   14 ____ light   19 ____ have
5 ____ wake   10 ____ board   15 ____ broad   20 ____ muse

47

Notice what happens
when you add **-ing** to these words:

dig—digging	hop—hopping	skip—skipping
beg—begging	stop—stopping	clap—clapping
run—running	shop—shopping	swim—swimming

Now look at the pictures and
find the missing words in the sentences.
Write them in the squares.

1 The girl is
2 The boys are
3 The frog is
4 The man is
5 The lady is
6 The dog is
7 The car is
8 The children are
9 The fish is

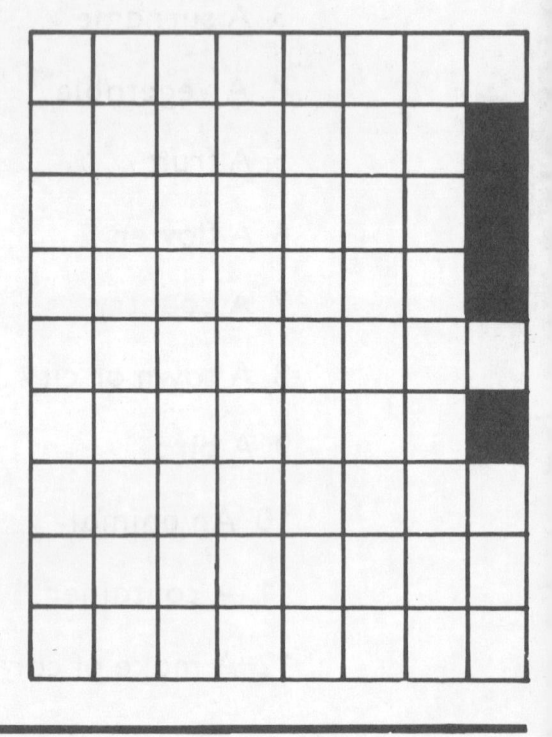

48

Find two little words in each big word.
Write them in the boxes, like this:

1 football	foot	ball	8 upstairs		
2 inside			9 downstairs		
3 outside			10 playground		
4 besides			11 anything		
5 tonight			12 nothing		
6 within			13 something		
7 without			14 bitten		

You need all of these words to solve the puzzles:

CURB   TURF   DEAF   HEAD   HAIRY   DREAD
CURL   HURT   BEAR   LAIR   DAIRY   DEATH

43

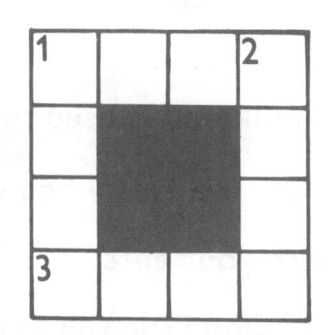

Across:
1 The part of the body that contains eyes and brain
3 Soil with grass roots growing in it
Down:
1 To cause pain or injury to
2 Unable to hear

44

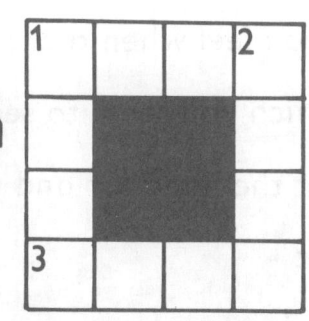

Across:
1 The chain under a horse's jaw to control it
3 A wild animal's den or resting place
Down:
1 Hair twisted into the shape of a screw
2 To put up with; to endure

45

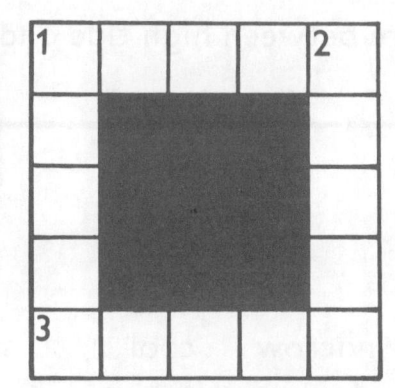

Across:
1 Great fear and anxiety
3 Covered with hair
Down:
1 The end of life
2 A building where milk is kept or sold

46

Write each of these words in the patch in front of the word nearest in meaning

dead	fair
ready	pair
steady	stair
surf	purse
burn	curse

1 _____ firm
2 _____ swear
3 _____ money-bag
4 _____ couple
5 _____ scorch
6 _____ lifeless
7 _____ blond
8 _____ step
9 _____ foam
10 _____ prepared

41

These are the words you need to solve this puzzle:

hear	rear	east	cream	beach
fear	tears	easy	dream	reach

1. It comes from milk and is used to make butter.
2. These come from the eyes when we cry.
3. You do this with your ears.
4. The opposite of west; the sun rises there
5. This is what you feel when there is danger.
6. Something which you seem to see during sleep.
7. To stretch out the hand for and take
8. The back part
9. Not difficult; simple
10. The shore between high tide and low tide

42

Choose from this list
the opposite of each word below.

right	firm	low	narrow	cool	start
tight	first	slow	shallow	sooner	partly
bright	dirty	below	hollow	foolish	sharp

opposite

1. clean
2. wrong
3. above
4. dull
5. high
6. loose

opposite

7. last
8. fast
9. wobbly
10. later
11. warm
12. blunt

opposite

13. wide
14. finish
15. deep
16. wise
17. solid
18. wholly

39

Can you solve this glidogram? Find the words in the list.

1	E						
2		E					
3			E				
4				E			
5					E		
6						E	
7					E		
8			E				
9		E					
10	E						
11	E						

50+30	THREE
30+40	SEVEN
Twice ten	ELEVEN
100−10	TWELVE
4+4+4+4	FIFTEEN
10×10	SIXTEEN
8+7	TWENTY
Half of six	SEVENTY
A dozen	EIGHTY
10−3	NINETY
5+6	HUNDRED

40

Beware! You only need eight of these words to solve the puzzle.

neat	frown	chain	mess	east
neatest	brown	sailing	bless	least
heater	flower	failing	press	beastly

1 The smallest in size or amount
2 Moving across sea or lake
3 To come into bloom
4 Something that warms the room up
5 Opposite the west
6 The most tidy
7 To make lines come on the forehead
8 To push steadily against

38

dive—diving	smile—smiling	ride—riding	chase—chasing
drive—driving	shine—shining	write—writing	shave—shaving
give—giving	phone—phoning	wave—waving	shake—shaking

You will find all the missing words in the list above:

1. The man in the first picture is —.
2. The man in the second picture is — a car.
3. The dog is — a cat.
4. The boy in the fourth picture is —.
5. Caroline is — the baby some food.
6. The lady in the sixth picture is — a mat.
7. The sun is —.
8. This boy is — good bye.
9. The girl in the ninth picture is —.
10. This girl is — a letter.
11. This boy is — his bicycle.
12. The lady in the last picture is — her friend.

36

Verbs add **-s** or **-es** in the same way as nouns:

I kick; he kicks   You teach; she teaches   You mix; he mixes
I pass; he passes   They wash; he washes   We fix; she fixes

Can you write the verb that is missing in each of these sentences?

1 I often brush my hair, and Anne often _____ hers too.

2 That is our dog barking. I'm afraid he often _____.

3 Gary often _____ television, and I often watch it too.

4 I don't mix the paints; Miss Green _____ them for me.

5 I often pass the ball, but he never _____ it.

6 I catch a bus every day, and Tom _____ the same bus.

37

You need all these words to solve this puzzle.

corn	fort	port	storm	cord
corner	forty	porter	stormy	cork

1 Very strong string

2 A town with a harbour

3 Wheat, oats, barley, maize, etc.

4 Ten more than thirty

5 You put it in a bottle to keep the air out

6 A person who earns his living by carrying bags

7 A period of rough wet weather

8 A place where two sides meet

9 A strong point built for defence

10 It is this when there are several storms.

33

When we want to make a noun mean more than one, we usually add **-s**, like this:
girl—girls, stamp—stamps.
But when the nouns end with s, x, sh, ch, we add **-es**, like this:
glass—glasses   brush—brushes
box—boxes   match—matches
When a noun means one, we call it singular.
Write the singular of each of the plural nouns in these lists.

Plural	Singular	Plural	Singular
1 dresses		9 posts	
2 frogs		10 patches	
3 foxes		11 pitches	
4 bushes		12 kisses	
5 straps		13 crashes	
6 dishes		14 messes	
7 classes		15 wishes	
8 cards		16 witches	

34

Write the plural of each of these singular nouns.
Can you spell all the words?

1 bus _____   5 pass _____   9 corner _____
2 box _____   6 brush _____   10 miss _____
3 stitch _____   7 catch _____   11 match _____
4 glass _____   8 scrap _____   12 bitch _____

35

Can you do laddergraphs?
You have to change one word into another by changing one letter at a time.
But each change must leave a real word.
The first has been done for you.

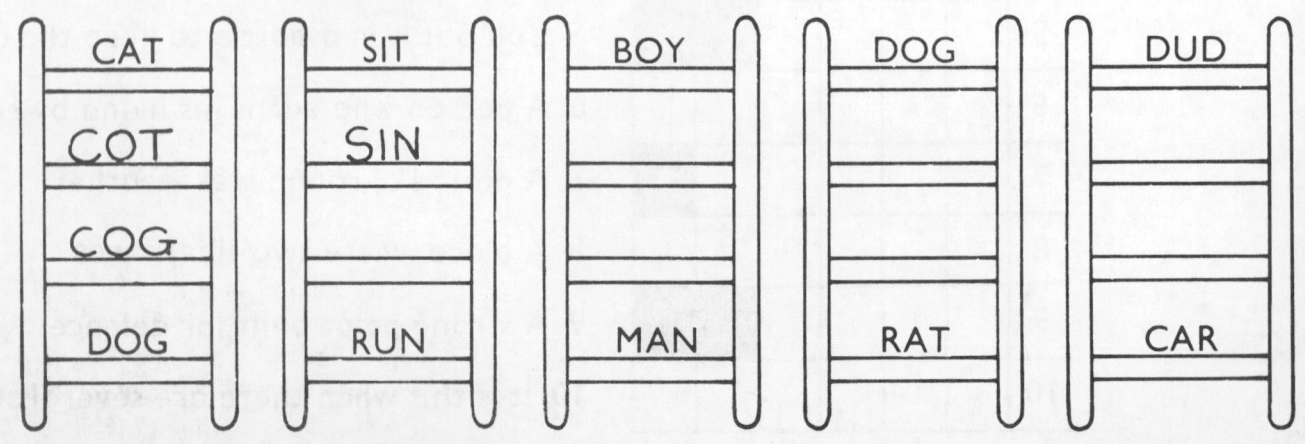

CAT	SIT	BOY	DOG	DUD
COT	SIN			
COG				
DOG	RUN	MAN	RAT	CAR

31

To solve this puzzle,
choose the right words from the list.

1. The opposite of soft
2. Land for raising crops or cattle
3. A building for storing corn or hay
4. You do this with a car
5. A spot
6. Land that belongs to a house
7. A place where you buy things
8. Crazy; mad
9. To mend a hole in your clothes
10. He raises crops or animals.
11. A small room for keeping food
12. A person who cuts hair and shaves

park
mark
market
hard
larder
garden
darn
barn
farm
farmer
barber
barmy

32

Can you solve this puzzle?
Check your answers with the Little Dictionary.

#							
1			A	R	T		To begin
2		A	R	T			A fruit pie
3			A	R	T		Clean and well dressed
4		A	R	T			Some, but not all of it
5		A	R	T			It is pulled by a horse
6			A	R	T		Aside
7		A	R	T			You throw it at a target
8		A	R	T			A sort of map
9				A	R	T	To leave

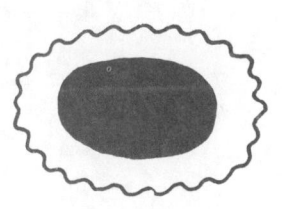

a tart

a dart

a cart

29

Each of these words has a double letter in it and ends with Y. Can you find them all? Check with the Little Dictionary.

#					
1			D	D	
2			N	N	
3			P	P	
4			R	R	
5			N	N	
6			R	R	
7			Z	Z	
8				B	B
9				T	T
10				T	T

1 Covered in mud
2 Full of sunshine
3 The opposite of sad
4 Feeling sad because you have done wrong
5 Comical
6 Covered in fur
7 Feeling as if your head were going round
8 Plump
9 Good-looking
10 Covered in spots

30

With the help of the Little Dictionary, write each of the words in the list in front of its meaning. Can you spell them all?

1 _____ much worn and perhaps faded   bossy

2 _____ messy; not done with care   mossy

3 _____ covered with moss   foggy

4 _____ having an unpleasant smell   boggy

5 _____ misty   knotty

6 _____ making too much fuss   sloppy

7 _____ full of knots   stubby

8 _____ marshy; wet and muddy   fussy

9 _____ full of small bubbles   fluffy

10 _____ short and thick   fizzy

11 _____ covered with fur or down   shabby

12 _____ too fond of giving orders   smelly

26

Which are hard and which are soft?
Put them in the right boxes.

| fork | paint | crab | balloon | bread | floor |
| pork | chain | moth | spoon | feathers | door |

soft things

1 _____ 4 _____
2 _____ 5 _____
3 _____ 6 _____

hard things

7 _____ 10 _____
8 _____ 11 _____
9 _____ 12 _____

27

Can you put in the missing word?
Beware! They do not all end in -ed.

1 I often paint pictures. I _____ one yesterday.

2 Mrs Wild often bolts her door. She _____ it last night.

3 John often swims. He _____ twice yesterday.

4 I often pass the salt. I _____ it just now.

5 Ann often folds her clothes. She _____ them last night.

6 Wayne often makes his own bed. He _____ it this morning.

7 I often hear a dog barking. I _____ one barking just now.

8 Mr Hunt often sells a cow. He _____ one last week.

28

Write each list in alphabetical order.
Can you spell the words?

1 sold _____   2 find _____   3 post _____
  scold _____   wind _____   most _____
  gold _____   blind _____   bolt _____
  hold _____   wild _____   colt _____
  fold _____   child _____   revolt _____

24

Write each of these names in front of its definition. Check with the Little Dictionary

dentist   jockey   docker   baker
artist   groom   cyclist miner

1. a person who draws or paints pictures
2. a person who makes and sells bread
3. a person who looks after your teeth
4. a man who loads or unloads ships
5. a person who looks after horses
6. a person who rides race-horses
7. a person who rides a bicycle
8. a man who digs coal, iron, etc., from the earth

25

Can you make words that end in **-er** from each of these? The word will name someone who does something. Check with the Little Dictionary.

1 talk   3 hunt   5 teach   7 earn   9 dive
2 walk   4 play   6 preach 8 learn 10 skate

1 talker, a person who talks
2
3
4
5
6
7
8
9
10

21

Read the sentences on the right, and then try to find the missing words in the sentences below.

Write them in the puzzle.

When I fall down I hurt myself.
When you fall down you hurt yourself.
When Tom falls down he hurts himself.
When Lesley falls down she hurts herself.
When we all fall down we all hurt ourselves.
When you and Bob fall down you hurt yourselves.
When people fall down they hurt themselves.

1 When Karen looks in the mirror she sees —.
2 When we look in the mirror we see —.
3 When I look in the mirror I see —.
4 When you look in the mirror you see —.
5 When Tony looks in the mirror he sees —.
6 When the boys look in the mirror they see —.
7 When you and Marion look in the mirror you see —.

22

A. Instead of **b** in **boss**, write:

1 t   2 m   3 l   4 cr

1 _____   3 _____
2 _____   4 _____

B. Instead of **p** in **pain**, write:

1 g   2 ch   3 r   4 ag

1 _____   3 _____
2 _____   4 _____

C. Instead of **k** in **keeping**, write:

1 cr   2 sl   3 p   4 w

1 _____   3 _____
2 _____   4 _____

23

Remove the first letter and write down the word that is left:

1 brain _____   3 laid _____   5 land _____
2 snail _____   4 again _____   6 sprinting _____

18

What are they doing?
Choose the right words from the list.
Write it under the picture.

landing	crashing	packing	catching	hanging
standing	splashing	quacking	scratching	banking

1 _____ 2 _____ 3 _____ 4 _____ 5 _____

6 _____ 7 _____ 8 _____ 9 _____ 10 _____

19

We make the word **splashing** from **splash**.
What do we make these words from?

1 catching _____ 3 lifting _____ 5 meeting _____

2 hanging _____ 4 sprinting _____ 6 keeping _____

20

Arrange each list in alphabetical order:

1 hunting _____   2 kicking _____   3 smelling _____

  grunting _____   licking _____   swelling _____

  rushing _____   sticking _____   sleeping _____

  brushing _____   pricking _____   peeping _____

  blushing _____   picking _____   spelling _____

16

| made | hate | bite | pipe | fine | tape | hope | slide |
| fade | rate | spite | ripe | shine | scrape | slope | hide |

What do you have to do
to make one of the words above
from each of the words below?
What happens to the sound of the word when you do this?
Write the words you make:

1 bit _bite_   5 rat _____   9 pip _____   13 slop _____

2 spit _____   6 hat _____   10 rip _____   14 hop _____

3 hid _____   7 fad _____   11 tap _____   15 shin _____

4 slid _____   8 mad _____   12 scrap _____   16 fin _____

17

Can you solve this puzzle?
Choose your words from these:

| mole | chime | blade | pale | wife |
| rope | wide | brake | cave | pile |

1 It's part of a knife and rhymes with made.
2 It's a kind of hole and rhymes with wave.
3 It stops you and rhymes with lake.
4 It is broad and rhymes with hide.
5 It lives under the ground and rhymes with hole.
6 It's a heap and rhymes with mile.
7 She has a husband and rhymes with life.
8 It's very thick string and rhymes with hope.
9 It is light in colour and rhymes with tale.
10 It comes from a clock and rhymes with slime.

15

Can you fit the four words into each word square? There is only one way of doing it. Here is a word square already filled in. →

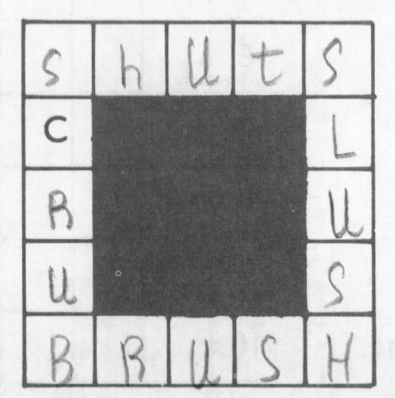

L	E	A	P
E			E
A			E
F	A	I	R

FAIR
LEAP
LEAF
PEER

1

h	a	n	g
e			a
a			n
R	a	n	g

RANG
HANG
HEAR
GANG

2

c	h	o	p
u			o
F			n
F	o	n	d

FOND
CHOP
CUFF
POND

3

M	E	S	S
I			O
S			M
S	A	L	E

SOME
SALE
MISS
MESS

4

S	h	u	t	S
C				L
R				U
U				S
B	R	U	S	H

BRUSH
SLUSH
SCRUB
SHUTS

5

B	O	R	N
I			I
F			C
F	A	C	E

FACE
NICE
BORN
BIFF

6

F	O	U	R
I			A
V			I
E	V	E	N

EVEN
FIVE
FOUR
RAIN

7

T	H	E	M
B			A
O			K
T	R	E	E

TROT
TREE
THEM
MAKE

8

S	T	O	O	D
H				R
O				I
O				V
K	N	I	F	E

SHOOK
STOOD
KNIFE
DRIVE

13

The first list is not in any special order,
but in the second list
the same words are in alphabetical order.
Peep comes before **seed**
because p comes before s in the alphabet.
Seed comes before **sheep**
because **e** comes before **h**.
If two words begin with the same letter.
you look at the second.
Can you write each of these lists in alphabetical order?

sheep	peep
weed	seed
peep	sheep
speed	sleep
seed	speed
sleep	weed

1 trick _____   2 sank _____   3 sack _____

  lick _____   tank _____   pack _____

  thick _____   swank _____   track _____

  sick _____   thank _____   slack _____

  stick _____   stank _____   tack _____

  tick _____   spank _____   smack _____

14

What is it?
The Little Dictionary will help.

Choose from this list:
↓

1 It squeaks and eats cheese. — donkey
2 It grunts and gives us pork. — bull
3 It brays and trots. — mouse
4 It bellows and charges. — snake
5 It quacks and waddles. — cock
6 It chatters and climbs trees. — duck
7 It crows and struts. — monkey
8 It hisses and glides. — deer
9 It howls and lopes. — wolf
10 It has antlers and runs very fast. — pig

10 These are the names of the things in the pictures.
Write them on their labels.

~~plate~~   ~~stamp~~   head   ~~brick~~   sack
~~date~~   ~~lamp~~   ~~bread~~ ~~chick~~ crack

1 chick
2 stamp
3 crack
4 lamp
5 date
6 plate
7 brick
8 bread
9 head
10 sack

11 Look at the pictures in 10 again.
Then cover up the pictures
and the words, and see how
many of the words you can write down.

1 chick   3 stamp   5 crack   7 lamp   9 date
2 plate   4 brick   6 bread   8 head   10 sack

12 Which words do these rhyme with?
Put them in the right boxes.

mend   rent   lend
sent   send   spelt
felt   melt   spent
tent   smelt   end

went	bend	belt
sent	mend	felt
tent	send	melt
rent	lend	smelt
spent	end	spelt

8

A. Instead of **w** in **wing**, write: 1 _sing_ 3 _thing_ 5 _string_
1 s 2 sl 3 th 4 sw 5 str 6 br   2 _sling_ 4 _swing_ 6 _bring_

B. Instead of **p** in **page**, write: 1 _rage_ 3 _wage_ 5 _savage_
1 r 2 c 3 w 4 st 5 sav 6 man   2 _cage_ 4 _stage_ 6 _manage_

C. Instead of **r** in **rock**, write: 1 ____ 3 ____ 5 ____
1 c 2 l 3 cl 4 s 5 bl 6 fr   2 ____ 4 ____ 6 ____

D. Instead of **l** in **lamp**, write: 1 ____ 3 ____ 5 ____
1 c 2 d 3 st 4 r 5 tr 6 cl   2 ____ 4 ____ 6 ____

E. Instead of **b** in **bump**, write: 1 ____ 3 ____ 5 ____
1 l 2 p 3 d 4 h 5 j 6 st   2 ____ 4 ____ 6 ____

F. Instead of **f** in **face**, write: 1 ____ 3 ____ 5 ____
1 r 2 l 3 p 4 pl 5 sp 6 tr   2 ____ 4 ____ 6 ____

9 Can you solve this puzzle?
You wrote all the words above.
If you fill in the puzzle correctly,
the second column down will spell
the name of something on your bed.
Check with the Little Dictionary.

1 There is nothing in this; it is emptiness.
2 A bird has one, and so has an aeroplane.
3 You tell the time with this.
4 A large solid piece of wood. It rhymes with rock.
5 You fasten doors with this.
6 A seat on ropes that goes up and down.

6

What do they rhyme with?
Choose from this list:

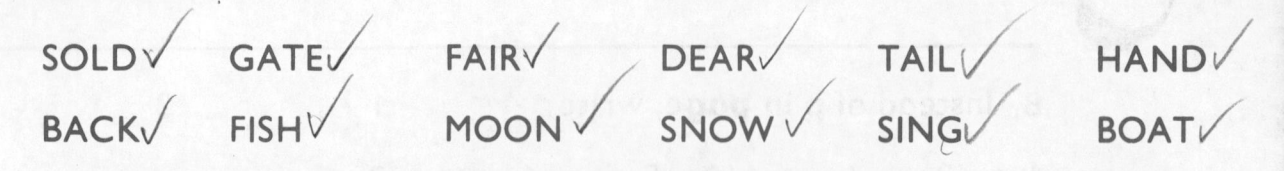

SOLD ✓ GATE ✓ FAIR ✓ DEAR ✓ TAIL ✓ HAND ✓
BACK ✓ FISH ✓ MOON ✓ SNOW ✓ SING ✓ BOAT ✓

1 LATE rhymes with GATE
2 HEAR rhymes with DEAR
3 GROW rhymes with SNOW
4 SACK rhymes with BACK
5 HAIR rhymes with FAIR
6 COLD rhymes with SOLD

7 WISH rhymes with FISH
8 FAIL rhymes with TAIL
9 SAND rhymes with HAND
10 COAT rhymes with BOAT
11 SOON rhymes with MOON
12 WING rhymes with SING

7

What is its opposite?
Choose from the list on the right of the puzzle.

#	word	answer	(crossed)
1	like	hate	~~slow~~
2	hot	cold	~~give~~
3	fast	slow	~~cold~~
4	push	pull	~~hate~~
5	thick	thin	~~late~~
6	cheap	dear	~~thin~~
7	wet	fine	~~dear~~
8	take	give	~~pull~~
9	early	late	~~fine~~
10	fair	dark	~~less~~
11	first	last	~~dark~~
12	more	less	~~last~~
13	long	short	~~sweet~~
14	strong	weak	~~deep~~
15	empty	full	~~awake~~
16	open	shut	~~short~~
17	asleep	awake	~~full~~
18	shallow	deep	~~never~~
19	sour	sweet	~~under~~
20	always	never	~~shut~~
21	nasty	nice	~~away~~
22	above	under	~~weak~~
23	up	down	~~nice~~
24	home	away	~~down~~

| 1 | shell / bell / well | 2 | ring / wing / king | 3 | quick / stick / lick | 4 | sweet / tree / sheep |
| 5 | rock / lock / clock | 6 | moon / boot / school | 7 | five / six / seven | 8 | cake / name / game |

4

Pick out and write down the word that belongs to the picture.

1 bell   3 stick   5 clock   7 five
2 king   4 sweet   6 boot   8 name

5

Can you find the missing words?
Choose them from the list on the right.
Write them in the puzzle.

1 We __ with our teeth.
2 We __ cars, buses, lorries.
3 We __ with a pen.
4 We __ ponies and bicycles.
5 We __ on ice.
6 You smell with your __.
7 A __ is an empty space.
8 You sometimes __ good-bye.
9 You __ through water.
10 We sometimes __ wild animals.
11 Some men __ their beards.
12 Some men __ pipes.

1	b	i	T	e	
2	d	r	i	v	e
3	a	r	i	t	e
4	r	i	d	e	
5	s	k	a	t	e
6	n	o	s	e	
7	h	o	l	e	
8	w	a	v	e	
9	w	a	d	e	
10	t	a	m	e	
11	s	h	a	v	e
12	s	m	o	k	e

write ✓
ride ✓
bite ✓
drive ✓
nose ✓
hole ✓
smoke
tame ✓
skate ✓
shave
wave ✓
wade

CAPITAL LETTERS
A B C D E F G H I J K L M N O P Q R S T U V W X Y Z

small letters
a b c d e f g h i j k l m n o p q r s t u v w x y z

1 Put in the missing letters of the alphabet:

| A | B | C | D | E | F | G | H | I | J | K | L | M | N | O | P | Q | R | S | T | U | V | W | X | Y | Z |
| A | B | c | D | e | F | G | h | i | j | K | L | m | n | O | P | q | R | S | t | u | V | w | x | y | z |

2 Copy the same words on to the other stairs, but in small letters.

1	O						
2	O	R					
3	O	R	E				
4	C	O	R	E			
5	S	C	O	R	E		
6	S	C	O	R	E	R	
7	S	C	O	R	I	N	G

1	o						
2	o	r					
3	o	r	e				
4	c	o	r	e			
5	s	c	o	r	e		
6	s	c	o	r	e	r	
7	s	c	o	r	i	n	g

3 Look at the first letter of each word. Write the words in the same order as the alphabet.

tore more horse good ear inside
bore core kite look yell queen
snore fly pipe nail jug zoo
wore dry arm rail old x-ray
              very
              under

1 arm   2 bore   3 core   4 dry   5 ear
6 fly   7 good   8 horse   9 inside   10 jug
11 kite   12 look   13 more   14 nail   15 old
16 pipe   17 queen   18 rail   19 snore   20 tore
21 under   22 very   23 wore   24 x-ray   25 yell   26 zoo

COLOUR IN THE NUMBER WHEN YOU HAVE ANSWERED THE QUESTION CORRECTLY.

Contents

- 1 The alphabet.
- 2 Small and capital letters.
- 3 Alphabetical order by first letter.
- 4 Revision of patterns from WORDS 1.
- 5 Revision of words with final e.
- 6 Revision by means of rhymes.
- 7 Revision by means of opposites.
- 8 Revision by means of initial consonants.
- 9 Revision by means of puzzle.
- 10 & 11 Revision by means of word game.
- 12 -end, -ent, -elt.
- 13 Alphabetical order by second letter.
- 14 Puzzle and use of dictionary.
- 15 Word squares: general revision.
- 16 & 17 final e.
- 18–20 Adding -ing.
- 21 Reflexive pronouns.
- 22 -oss, -ain, -eeping.
- 23 Revision of ai.
- 24 & 25 Doers: -ist, -er.
- 26 Hard and soft objects: consolidation.
- 27 Adding -ing, -ed.
- 28 -old, -olt, -ost, -ind, -ild.
- 29 & 30 Adjectives ending in -y with double consonant.
- 31 & 32 ar.
- 33 & 34 Plurals -es.
- 35 Laddergraphs.
- 36 Verb endings changing to -es.
- 37 or.
- 38 Adding -ing to verbs ending in e.
- 39 Numbers.
- 40 ea, ow, ai, ess.
- 41 -ea.
- 42 Opposites.
- 43–46 ur, air, ea.
- 47 Adding -ing and doubling consonant.
- 48 Compound words.
- 49 Revision games.
- 50 Initial a-, be-.
- 51 Adding -ed and doubling consonant.
- 52 Collective nouns.
- 53 ie, ew (lies, blew).
- 54 Short fat or long thin things.
- 55 oi.
- 56 -er, est, -en and double consonant.
- 57 Verbs: consolidation.
- 58 Plurals -ies.
- 59 Verb endings that change to -ies, -ied.
- 60 Rhymes.
- 61 Puzzle for consolidation. The Little Dictionary.

LONGMAN

ALL ROUND ENGLISH
WORDS
2

dead
ready   fair
steady   pair
surf   stair
burn   purse
         curse

1 You
2 You
3 You

kettles of water.

ropes to store them.

RONALD RIDOUT